Failure to Launch

Failure to Launch

Guiding Clinicians to Successfully Motivate the Long-Dependent Young Adult

By Michael D. DeVine, MS, LPC-S

With Contributions by
Lawrence V. Tucker, MD

JASON ARONSON
Lanham • Boulder • New York • Toronto • Plymouth, UK

Published by Jason Aronson
A wholly owned subsidiary of The Rowman & Littlefield Publishing Group, Inc.
4501 Forbes Boulevard, Suite 200, Lanham, Maryland 20706
www.rowman.com

10 Thornbury Road, Plymouth PL6 7PP, United Kingdom

Copyright © 2013 by Jason Aronson

All rights reserved. No part of this book may be reproduced in any form or by any electronic or mechanical means, including information storage and retrieval systems, without written permission from the publisher, except by a reviewer who may quote passages in a review.

British Library Cataloguing in Publication Information Available

Library of Congress Cataloging-in-Publication Data
DeVine, Michael D., 1979–
Failure to launch : guiding clinicians to successfully motivate the long-dependent young adult / by Michael D. DeVine, MS, LPC-S ; with contributions by Lawrence V. Tucker, MD.
pages cm
Includes bibliographical references and index.
ISBN 978-0-7657-0955-4 (cloth : alk. paper)—ISBN 978-0-7657-0956-1 (electronic)
1. Motivation (Psychology) in adolescence. 2. Dependency (Psychology) 3. Young adults—Psychology. I. Title.
BF724.3.M65D48 2013
155.6'5825—dc23
2013008928
ISBN 978-1-4422-5082-6 (pbk : alk. paper)

∞™ The paper used in this publication meets the minimum requirements of American National Standard for Information Sciences Permanence of Paper for Printed Library Materials, ANSI/NISO Z39.48-1992.

Printed in the United States of America

Contents

Introduction	vii
I: Background and Theory	**1**
1 What Is Failure to Launch?	3
2 "Twenty-two Is the New Eighteen"	11
3 So Are They Narcissistic, Entitled, or Just a Bunch of A$!hol&s?	23
4 The Loving Enabler	31
II: Underlying Mental Health Issues	**39**
5 Mood Disorders and Anxiety	41
6 Attention Deficit Hyperactivity Disorder	51
7 Pervasive Developmental Disorders	61
8 Substance Abuse	69
III: Moving the Immovable Object	**79**
9 Why Change? What's My Motivation to Change?	81
10 "What Do You Want to Do Now That You Are Grown Up?"	91
11 Career and Life Coaching	101
12 Empowering the Family	111
IV: It's Now Up to the Family	**119**
13 Preparing for Launch	121
14 The Launch Pad	135
15 Clearing the Tower	143

| **16** Houston, We Have a Problem | 151 |
| **17** Houston, We Have Liftoff | 157 |

Afterword	163
References	165
Index	167
About the Authors	175

Introduction

When I begin to read a book by a fellow colleague in this field, I usually pick the book because they are an expert in the field on the topic. They usually know more than anybody else in the field and have seen hundreds of clients with this particular problem. Their knowledge and experience allows them to explain to fellow clinicians how to work with their own clients. While I believe that my training, expertise, and clinical experience qualify me to write this book, there is one other major reason that qualifies me to write this book: I was once a failure to launch adult–child myself.

When I was a young adolescent in high school, I struggled with low motivation and I did just enough work to stay out of trouble. I barely studied for my tests, turned in sloppy homework, and rarely wrote papers without asking my father to write them for me. Even though my parents were paying for me to have flying lessons, I never studied for my FAA test and only put in the minimal effort necessary to keep my flight instructor off of my back. My parents rarely said anything to me about my grades, so I figured if I could get away with doing nothing, why should I put in more effort?

During my senior year I started smoking pot with my friends and probably put more time and effort into that than preparing for the SAT or applying to college. As my senior year wound down, I started to become wary about being a pilot. The truth of the matter was that I had no confidence in myself to succeed as a pilot and it seemed just too difficult to get my license and continue my studies at an aeronautical school.

I had slacked off so much in high school that I realized that when I really wanted to try, I had no idea of how to be a student or even know how to study. After failing my first FAA practice exam, I decided that being a pilot was not for me and withdrew my acceptance to college and quit flying all together.

My parents were very disappointed with my decision, but they felt as though they had no power over the situation and let me back down without any fight at all. I graduated high school with a 2.29 GPA and was given a delayed spring acceptance to Ohio State University. After graduation, I had no idea what I wanted to do with my life, so I decided to do what I knew best—partying with my friends as much as I could. I lived with my parents at the time, and as long as I worked part-time, I was allowed to live at home. So I worked part-time and tried not to come home too late every night.

When school started in the fall, I did not take my classes seriously, and I skipped more classes than I went to. I rarely looked at my class syllabus, and I did not turn in half of my school work. I failed most of my classes that quarter, and I swore to my parents that I would start to do better when I went to Ohio State University in the spring. As I am sure you have already guessed, I just partied with my old friends and all the new friends that I met at Ohio State. I failed two classes and even got a D in the study skills class.

My parents took me out of Ohio State and told me that I had one more quarter to figure out what I wanted to do with myself or they were not going to pay for college anymore. While most people would think that failing your entire first year of college would provide some motivation, in my case it did not. I continued to just hang out and party with my friends for the first few weeks of summer before I had an epiphany.

I was at a friend's graduation party drinking a few beers out front with my friend Andy. The thing you have to understand about Andy was that, while he partied as much as I did, he actually went to school and attained excellent grades at a local private school. Andy and I just were hanging out, talking about people, life, politics, and so forth. When he asked me what I was going to do with my life. He said something along the lines of, "How could a kid as smart as you get such crappy grades?" He went on to call me the dumbest smart kid that he ever has known.

What Andy said to me really struck a chord because I really started to think about what I was doing with my life. I told Andy that night that I needed to figure my life out, stop talking about how smart I was and actually show people in school how smart I was. I said that since we are always talking about why people do what they do, why not go into psychology? So starting the next semester, I changed my major to psychology and started taking school seriously. Was it easy? Not the least bit. I had to learn how to study, write papers, organize, do homework, and so forth for the very first time in my life. I even had my freshman English teacher sit down with me after class for two weeks and teach me how to write a standard English essay paper.

It was also difficult to study downstairs while my friends were upstairs drinking, or to tell them I could not go out that night because I had a test the next day. It was such a culture shock to me and actually caused me a lot of mental pain to sit through an entire class and take notes. But because I discovered what I wanted to do with my life, I was able to deal with that pain and make the changes that were necessary. I got a 4.0 GPA that fall semester and eventually transferred over to the same private school that my friend, Andy, was going to in the fall. My parents were still cautious with me and said that if my grades were not in the 3.0 or above range, they would take me out of the school, which was a very good thing because it kept me honest about studying.

I overcame all of my problems, and I was able to launch myself in to my own future. Of course, I made my journey more difficult by waiting until I was twenty to start doing well in school, but I finally figured it out.

For those of you who have known me for many years, you have all heard my story and even make jokes about my past experiences (such as going to over twenty Dave Matthews Band concerts). The jokes do not bother me because they are quite funny. But for those of you just now getting to know me through this book, I want you to understand that I am not just defining and explaining this problem through the eyes of a clinician, but also as a thirty-three-year-old adult, who has had time to look back at his past and used it to define a current problem. While I do not believe that I had to go through the things that I did as a young adult to write this book, those experiences helped me define it in a different light and have allowed me to work with my clients on a different level.

I believe the information in this book will help your clients. I hope that my own experiences with this very problem will help you understand your clients better and help you relate to them on a different level.

I

Background and Theory

Chapter One

What Is Failure to Launch?

I swear, if he fails one more class I am going to bounce him out the front door faster than next semester's tuition check.

—Anonymous parent

If you are reading this book right now, chances are you have heard a parent say this very phrase or something similar to it. There is perhaps nothing more frustrating to a parent than to spend hard-earned money educating a child who does not seem to appreciate the education in the first place. Every day in my practice, a parent comes through the door pleading for help to figure out why his or her child does not seem motivated to do well in school, or in life in general, for that matter. Most parents have been dealing with this problem for several years and have finally reached their boiling point by the time they decide to seek outside help. Understandably, many are irate or just plain exhausted from endless fights with their children and strings of broken promises such as "next semester I am really going to buckle down and study."

This is not just a problem with college students, but young adult children in general. Many parents describe how their children just did not have the motivation to go to school, so they are working a minimum wage job, living at home, and playing Xbox until 5:00 a.m. every day. One parent recently asked me, "Michael, how do you motivate a child who is perfectly happy with doing absolutely nothing?"

Growing up I heard stories from my parents about how, when they turned eighteen, they were either forced to go into a family business, drafted into a war, or chose to go to college on their own dime. My parents were twenty-two when they had my sister, and my father was working full-time and going to night school for his MBA. I, on the other hand, at age twenty-two, was a junior in college and barely able to take care of my laundry and study for finals exams at the same time. My idea of grocery shopping was going to my parents' house on Sunday and raiding their refrigerator for whatever handout my mother would give me.

Times have changed incredibly from my parents' day, but they also have changed since I was twenty-two. It appears that twenty-one is the new eighteen. Instead of feeling the pressure to go out and make their own place in the world, kids are perfectly happy without cutting the umbilical cord until the very last minute. While my cohorts and I were a bit slow to learn how to grocery shop and do our own laundry, we still had a desire to do well in this world, and we did well in school without being bribed or threatened by our parents to do so. We learned to set our own course and sail independently into our future; it was just at a slower rate than our predecessors. Now we have an entire generation of children who have failed to set a course altogether and feel no remorse or guilt about it at all. This is what we have coined as "failure to launch."

What makes this problem so difficult is that there is not a single reason for why this phenomenon occurs. Many parents and clinicians believe that failure to launch into a life independent of the family is unique to entitled and narcissistic children who have no problem wasting their youth or their parents' resources. In reality, many more factors come into play.

As a licensed professional counselor in a large clinic outside of Dallas, I'm able to utilize SPECT brain imaging (Single Photon Emission Computed Tomography) as a tool to diagnosis and treat mental illnesses. With this tool, we attract a large population of clients who typically have seen other clinicians with multiple conflicting diagnoses or have been to several therapists without any positive change. By the time most of our clients have found us, they are mentally exhausted, out of answers, and, in many cases, ready to give up on their children.

Parents want simple answers to fix their children, but unfortunately the problem is multifaceted and requires a parent and clinician to evaluate each situation to determine the true etiology of the issue. In my practice, I typically see clients who fall into four major categories, with several clients sharing characteristics of all four.

The first type of client falls into the category of what most parents would label as lazy, entitled, or completely unmotivated. Take the following case for example:

Mrs. Smith and her husband walked into my office with a painful scowl on each of their faces. My schedule indicated that I was meeting with a nineteen-year-old client, but notably absent from my office was the nineteen-year-old. Instead, I had two parents who stated with intense sarcasm, "We're sorry, John is not here today. He played Xbox until 4:00 a.m. last night, and when we tried to wake him up at 10:00 for our appointment today, he refused to get up, told us to go away, and that we needed therapy—not him."

When I asked Mr. and Mrs. Smith why they were in my office today, they explained that John had failed most of his classes during his freshman year and was put on academic probation for his entire sophomore year. During the summer between his freshman and sophomore years, John and his parents reached an agreement about his grades and that he would pay them $100/$200 for every C/D he got in the fall semester, and they would give him $200/$100 for every A/B that he earned. John swore up and down that he was going to do better this semester and promised to seek help if he got into trouble again.

Throughout the entire semester, John had promised his parents that he was doing well and turning in all his work. They had just received his grades for the fall semester, and he failed one class, received one D, and dropped two other classes earlier in the year because he was going to fail them. John's parents pulled him out of the university and enrolled him in a local community college for the spring semester to get his grades up. Only instead of getting his grades up, he began hanging out with his friends, playing video games, and barely making it to his classes every day. Mr. and Mrs. Smith said that they were beside themselves about what to do with their son. They were concerned because he seemed completely happy with not finishing college and living at home for the rest of his life.

Patients such as this usually come in to our clinic for some sort of ADHD or learning disability assessment, because the parents have tried everything in their arsenal to motivate their child without success. The next logical conclusion is that the child must have something mentally wrong with him or her. In cases such as these, there usually is not a developmental history of ADHD or learning disabilities, and the SPECT scans show a completely normal brain. As clinicians, this tells us that this problem is 100 percent behavioral/psychological and the work needs to be done with the parents and the children.

The second type of client falls into the category of what we determine to be directionless or having no idea what he or she wants to do with his or her life. Let's face it, we may love our careers, but I know I did not enjoy sitting through a class studying fourteenth-century European history. We studied hard because we knew we had to get an A in order to get into our choice of medical schools or graduate school programs. Imagine putting up with four years of classes when you have no end goal, no career chosen, and no foreseeable light at the end of the tunnel. To illustrate, take a look at the following case:

Kevin was a twenty-three-year-old male who was referred to our clinic by his father. Kevin's dad had hopes that his son would finally get his act together and figure out what he wanted to do with his life. Kevin tried going to community college several times, but became bored with the material and would drop out before finishing the semester.

Kevin had mild ADHD and was taking his medication regularly, but even that could not get him to finish even one semester of college. He floundered from one failed career choice to the next until his father finally threatened to cut him off unless he got help. Kevin was a smart kid, but he had no idea what he wanted to do with his life. One day it was a race car driver; the next day it was a financial advisor or a musician. All Kevin knew is that he wanted to be rich and was just waiting on something to happen.

After doing some intensive career exploration, including vocational assessment, all of Kevin's testing indicated that his true passion and interests were in the music field, so together we explored all the possible career options in that field. Kevin was not aware of the different options available to him and realized that a career in music production and technology was something that he could have a lot of enthusiasm for. Several local universities offered excellent music programs and, after five years of several failed college attempts, Kevin is now going to school, excelling, and is pursuing his bachelor's degree in music.

Patients such as Kevin are typically good kids, but they are generally just lost. They need some direction in their lives so they can rationalize why they are putting themselves through the pain of an education. Furthermore, these clients struggle to justify embarking on a journey, where they have no idea where they are going. To us, it's like going on a road trip across the country and having no destination picked out. Where do you start? What roads do you use? Is that a trip you would make?

The third type of patient falls into the category of having some sort of undiagnosed mental health disorder. One of the most frequent concerns we see in our clinic is very intelligent children who made their way through high school with excellent grades, but somehow started to falter once in college. At one point they were highly-motivated students who lived and breathed studying, but now they have become defeated, unmotivated, pessimistic college students who would rather stay in their dorm rooms all day than go to class. Typically these students were never tested in high school because of their intelligence, but once they were put under any type of increased academic stress, underlying problems that never surfaced now cause chaos.

Howard was described by his parents as a straight-A student in high school who had high hopes of becoming the next Bill Gates. He was accepted into a prestigious private university, and his parents sent him off to college without a single concern about his ability to succeed.

Howard's parents became concerned halfway through his first semester when he started failing his classes. He offered very little explanation as to why he was struggling with academics for the first time in his life. Howard failed two of his classes during his first semester and did even worse his second semester. When Howard was placed on academic probation, his parents were informed that he was not going to several of his classes and that he did not ask for any additional help or tutoring. During the summer, his parents tried to confront him about why he was not going to class. Howard's response was one of remorse, and he promised to start figuring out how to handle stress better.

When Howard went back to school the following fall, his parents decided to surprise him at school and, instead of surprising him after class, they discovered him in his dorm playing games on his computer. Howard's parents pulled him out of school and decided to cancel the next semester's tuition.

Desperate to find some answers, Howard was brought into our clinic. He told his story of feeling intense social anxiety, as soon as he started school, and only made friends with people whom he played games with online. As he started to become overwhelmed with his coursework, his anxiety grew more severe and he felt ashamed about asking for help. It became easier to avoid his professors altogether rather than ask for help or face another failed exam. After an extensive clinical interview with Howard and his parents, plus a SPECT brain scan, we discovered that Howard was struggling with undiagnosed ADHD and also had several features of Asperger's syndrome.

Howard's story is more common than you might think. So many times a client will display very subtle symptoms of ADHD, depression, anxiety, and Asperger's when they are growing up. It is not until their systems are stressed (i.e., being away from home; experiencing new environments at school or work; lacking friends, etc.), that the symptoms become severe enough for others to see and for it to affect their academic performance. Unfortunately, many times these clients are away from the people who love and know them best, and problems go undetected until they come home for the holidays or even the following year. Sometimes all it takes is one semester for a child to display some significant changes in his or her mental state.

The last type of patient falls into the category of enabling family systems. Most clients who walk into our doors are loving parents who have the best intentions for their children. They want to see their children succeed and will do everything in their power to ensure that they do, even at the cost of not allowing them to fail. One of the biggest mistakes parents make is seeing their children experiencing problems with focus, motivation, or happiness. When the problem continues for an extended time period, they start to panic and try everything they can do to fix it.

Typically what happens in this situation is that the child is not allowed to fail, and he or she starts to lose any incentives to actually succeed. Picture yourself as a twenty-one-year-old student who lives at home rent-free, is not made to work, is given an allowance, has no bills, has a free car, and goes out drinking with your friends several times per week on your parents' dime. Sounds like a pretty great life, doesn't it? Why on earth would you want to change that?

Parents often come into our clinic and say that their child is lost and they have no idea what to do. They say things such as, "He is an adult. What can I really do?" When we ask them why they continue to pay for all of these things and support their child even though he is not living up to his end of the bargain, our favorite answer is, "What if we kick him out and he becomes homeless?"

It is this very line of thinking that powers the enabling cycle and prevents parents from setting the boundaries that can force their children to take action. Many of these parents are anxiety-ridden about their lack of power in the situation when, in fact, they have all of the power in the world. Let's take a look at Bobby.

Bobby was a bright-eyed young eighteen-year-old with high hopes of majoring in drama and possibly pursuing a career in acting. He was accepted into one of the most competitive drama programs in the country and was eager to begin his career. Soon after getting to college, Bobby started hanging out with a group of students who were into partying. He soon became the go-to guy for booze in his dorm.

What started out as a social activity soon became an almost daily occurrence. Bobby started skipping classes and soon was suspended from school for drinking in his dorm, along with several other infractions. His parents brought him home after one semester with hopes that they would be able to better control his behavior. They tried to reach an agreement that revolved around his getting his grades up in community college and then transferring back to his school the following year.

Shortly after coming home, Bobby started hanging out with a new group of friends that he met at work. He began going out every night and also heavily abusing cocaine. He came home almost every night at dawn and often got into screaming matches with his parents. He lost his job, wrecked his parents' car, and quit going to school. Yet his parents continued to let him live at home, supported him financially, and even bought him a new car which he wrecked while driving intoxicated.

By the time his parents came into our clinic, Bobby had a significant drug problem, was refusing any type of treatment, and his family feared for his safety. When asked what they were willing to do to fix the problem, his mother replied, "What can we do? He is an adult."

While on paper the answer to her statement would seem obvious, but for parents in this situation, the answer is not remotely as clear. Whether you have a child who is faltering and abusing drugs or just faltering and living on your couch, it is a scary situation for anyone. The parent's love for the child—plus a hesitation to inflict any additional pain—blinds him or her from the truth. The truth is that parents are major contributors to the problem and have all the power in the world to change the situation. But change is much easier in theory than in reality.

When we sit down with parents and begin to explain to them our clinical impressions and outline why their children have failed to launch, we are met with many different reactions. Some parents look at each other and become even more defeated and blame themselves for being ineffective parents. Some parents get defensive and try to explain why they made their decisions.

Particularly in cases of undiagnosed mental health problems, many parents show complete surprise as to how badly their child was struggling and had no idea that certain mental illnesses could wreak havoc in their child's life. Many of these same parents will retrospectively look back at their child's behavior and have those "ah-ha" moments—when all of a sudden, they realize that the signs and symptoms were there all along and they just never put two and two together.

Regardless of the situation or the reaction, the answer and treatment plan remains the same. This book is the culmination of my knowledge of counseling theory, family systems theory, psychiatry, and cutting-edge neurological research to give you every tool that you need. What you will find in the pages that follow is the information to help you define why this problem is occurring and what possible underlying psychological conditions could be exacerbating this problem. Furthermore, the following chapters will not only help you identify the problem, but will also walk you through step-by-step instructions on how you can help your clients through this problem. By the time you are done reading this book, you will have a definitive plan on how to help launch your clients off of their parent's couch and into *their* future.

If you are dealing with a "failure to launch" client, I encourage you to turn the page and learn what you can do to help them succeed.

Chapter Two

"Twenty-two Is the New Eighteen"

One evening, when I was twenty-one years old, I came home from my part-time job as a pizza delivery man, and my mom called me to ask if I wanted to come over for dinner. I clearly remember my parents being on speaker phone when they called, and I went on a diatribe about how I couldn't come over for dinner because I was exhausted and had so much homework to do for my cognitive psychology class.

I remember saying how cruel the professor was, and how he must hate his students because it was impossible to complete everything that he wanted, and still work a part-time job, in addition, to having fun with my friends. After finishing my rant, all I could hear was my father mocking me in the background—the sound of him playing a violin as background for my pity party. He simply told me that I had no idea what stress was and that I should try working full-time, going to school at night, being a husband, and raising a child. I did not have a response to that and simply said that I would be over for dinner in twenty minutes.

Now, I understand that everybody within ten years of my age has heard something similar from their parents. The standard comeback from parents of having to walk to school in ten feet of snow both ways is also well-documented. But despite our parents' overdramatizations of their young adulthood, they actually are more on target than they realize.

When you review the data, there has been a dramatic shift in the lives of eighteen- to twenty-two-year-olds in the 1960s/1970s compared to the same young adults today. In the 1960s, the average age of marriage was twenty-three years old for men and twenty years old for women. Starting in the 1990s, the average age people married, began a career, and started a family shifted dramatically to twenty-six years old for men and twenty-four years old for women. Then, in 2000, those numbers continued to climb to twenty-seven years old for men and twenty-five years old for women. When you look at the data, it is quite clear that our parents knew what they were talking about. It's taken our generation a full five years longer to mature into adulthood!

So why is this happening? Are we just that much lazier than our parents? The simple answer is no. Life has changed dramatically in the past forty years. When my parents were eighteen, they were simply pushed out of the house and given little to no support as they transitioned from adolescence to adulthood. They were faced with a rather grim reality: do as their parents told them to do or good luck in adulthood. When my father was eighteen, he was faced with a rather limited decision: go to school or be drafted into the Vietnam War.

My father, in complete defiance to his parents, decided to enlist in the U.S. Army and go off to war. My mother had few options herself: either go to school to be a nurse or stay at home and live with her parents. The baby-boomer generation entered the world on their own. For them, it was either sink or swim into adulthood. Today, the biggest decisions most eighteen-year-olds make are: What college should I go to or what should my major be?

When my parents were twenty-two, they determined how to make ends meet while raising their first child and educating themselves so they could get better/higher paying jobs. Most twenty-two-year-olds today try to find their first job or determine what graduate school they want to apply to.

Instead of being forced into adulthood immediately when they turn eighteen, most kids today enter into a period of *Emerging Adulthood*. This term was first phrased by Jeffrey Arnett, PhD, in an attempt to explain the changing demographics of the eighteen- to twenty-two-year-old group. Instead of going right into adulthood, they enter into emerging adulthood, where they slowly transition into the concept of being an independent adult.

Many factors played into this changing demographic, according to Dr. Arnett. First and foremost, the rise of the use of birth control in the '60s/'70s. Instead of having your first child accidentally, soon after marriage, couples were able to better plan for their first child—opting rather to wait until their careers and finances were more secure.

Secondly, the importance of college began to change and, whereas once it was considered a privilege of a lucky few to go to college, by the 1990s it became a rite of passage for high school graduates to attend college—almost two-thirds of all eighteen-year-olds. Furthermore, the length of an education grew to a mean of four years, with many kids taking five or even six years to attain their bachelor's degrees. With as many as one-third of all college students deciding now to attain advanced degrees, you find kids spending anywhere from an additional two years to as many as eight extra years of postgraduate schooling.

During the baby-boomer generation, most people would answer that marriage and family were major goals in their early adulthood. But today most people aged eighteen to twenty-two would rather name this as an impediment to adulthood.

So what makes up this new age group of emerging adulthood? Arnett characterized it into five parts:

1. It is the age of identity exploration: trying out new possibilities in areas such as love and work.
2. It is the age of instability.
3. It is the most self-focused age of life.
4. It is the age of feeling in between, in transition, neither being an adolescent nor being an adult.
5. It is the age of possibilities, when hopes flourish, when people have unparalleled opportunity to transform their lives.

When breaking down emerging adulthood, one has to take a step back and realize how good the Gen Xs (those people born from mid-'60s to early-'80s) had it and how every generation following (Gens Y and Z and Millennials) should be thankful. We were given an opportunity to fully self-actualize ourselves without the pressure of a draft or parents who were pushing us out the door. What the idea of emerging adulthood really is . . . it's a gift from the baby boomers.

While researching this book, I had a great conversation with my father over coffee. I asked him why his generation decided to approach life differently than his parents, and his answer was very telling. To boil it down, he said that it was an awful and scary feeling to be thrust into the world at eighteen. The world was changing quickly and much of the innocence from "the greatest generation" (pre–baby-boomer population) had waned, and they inherited a much scarier world—where you either found a way to fly on your own or the world swallowed you up.

Furthermore, my father said that the early 1960s was not a very nurturing time to explore your true desires. If you wanted to be an artist or a college English professor, you were told that it was rubbish and you would never support a family on a pipe dream such as that. You were usually given an ultimatum, as in my father's experience, and you either did what your parents wanted you to do or you were on your own. My father expanded and said that when it came time for the baby boomers to raise their own children, they realized the importance of letting a child live out his dreams and live up to his full potential.

Where practicality and dollars and cents ruled the day of my parents' generation, my generation valued happiness and passion for one's career. So instead of throwing their children to the wolves, my father said that his generation vowed to work as hard as they could, make as much money as possible, and give their children the love, support, and time to figure what they wanted to do—thus sparing my generation the anguish of what he'd experienced. Much like the "greatest generation" gave their children and communities the infrastructure to take the country into the future, the baby-boomer generation gave us emerging adulthood for our own happiness.

I was really taken aback by my father's frankness on the topic. I guess I thought the concept of the emerging adult kind of happened accidentally—rather than the product of a fast-changing world. But my father gave me a totally new perspective on the topic. Now, I do understand that this theory is just my father's and does not speak for an entire generation, but it really made sense to me and made me feel even luckier to have been given the opportunity to flounder for two years while I transitioned from the idea of being a pilot to finding my true passion as a counselor.

So where, exactly, did everything go wrong? How did we take a parental gift that allowed eighteen- to twenty-two-year-olds the time to explore, mature, and self-actualize and turn it into a period where many kids failed to launch completely. Instead, they became mired in arrested development?

Consider this saying that I heard a lot while growing up: "The road to hell is paved with good intentions." Starting in the 1970s, something called the self-esteem movement started to take hold in schools across the country. The self-esteem movement was an offshoot of humanistic psychology which was started by Carl Rogers and Abraham Maslow. Carl Rogers (1951) defined self-esteem as: "Every human being, with no exception, for the mere fact to be it, is worthy of unconditional respect of everybody else; he deserves to esteem himself and to be esteemed."

Roy F. Baumeister, Jennifer D. Campbell, Joachim I. Krueger, and Kathleen D. Vohs (2005) discuss that within this movement was the basic and innocent concept that we should be doing everything in our power as teachers, coaches, and parents to build up a child's self-esteem. Instead of having classrooms with demerits and posted grades to foster competition, we were encouraged to implement charts that listed how many warm fuzzies were earned for the week. Instead of red ink smattered across a paper or test, motivational tools such as happy face stickers with "keep trying" and other uplifting phrases were used.

It really was an innocent movement. Why would we *not* want to make our children feel good about themselves? This is not a rhetorical question that I intend to purposely leave open, rather a facetious attempt to point out the glaring weakness of the movement. That weakness being that the self-esteem movement has been hypothesized by psychologists to not only inflate a child's self-worth, but rather to also artificially inflate their *sense* of self-worth. Instead of teaching children a lesson about making mistakes and learning how to work harder, it became more about not allowing a child to fail and only reinforcing the idea that the final result is all that matters (i.e., getting the positive reinforcement).

Interestingly enough, recent studies looked at comparing American students to Japanese students in the realm of cheating in school. The results of the study determined that American students were more likely to cheat because it was only the final result that mattered, and cheaters were absolved of guilt because the ends justified the means. Their Japanese cohorts reported profoundly less incidents of cheating and related that it was the main product of the Japanese culture that reinforced effort and valuing effort over the end result (Lupton, Chapman, & Weiss, 2000).

In addition to work ethic, one of the most hotly contested results of the self-esteem movement is narcissism. Narcissism is defined in Webster's dictionary as "an inordinate fascination with oneself; excessive self-love; vanity." In short, narcissism in very small doses is actually a good thing, but when it becomes so overwhelmingly part of someone's life, then it is maladaptive and can cause significant problems.

Starting in 1982, a group of researchers at San Diego State University led by Jean Twinge, PhD, author of *Generation Me and The Narcissism Epidemic*, gave incoming freshmen the Narcissism Personality Inventory (NPI) and tracked the results through 2006. During that time, over 16,475 college students were inventoried, and the results were rather stunning. Their results showed a consistent trend of increasing rates of narcissism all the way up through 2006. The stunning part was that it was not by a small amount. By 2006, two-thirds of college freshman reported 30 percent higher levels of narcissism than the college students in 1982. Dr. Twinge, in her study, stated that "we need to stop endlessly repeating 'You're special' and having children repeat that back. Kids are self-centered enough already."

As I wrote earlier, small levels of narcissism are a good thing—which was probably the main goal of the self-esteem movement. But high levels of narcissism can lead to significant problems for society and kids, such as poor/short-term romantic relationships, lack of empathy, egocentric thinking, lack of emotional warmth, superficial relationships, quid pro quo relationships, game playing, overcontrolling behaviors, and violent behaviors.

How many parents right now reading this book have seen some if not all of these behaviors in their kids who have failed to launch? I can confidently say that the majority of parents who bring in their children to our clinic have the most of these symptoms. So many, in fact, that most parents interpret these symptoms/traits as indicators of some underlying psychological condition—basically saying, "There is no way my kid can be this self-centered, so he must have ADHD or something psychologically wrong with him."

The truth of the matter is that a good portion of our clients do not have any significant underlying psychological conditions that are causing their arrested development. The problem really is good old-fashioned narcissism.

The research backs up everything that I see in my practice, and if you really take a good hard look at your child, the answer is pretty obvious.

A good portion of our clients come from families of means, and many of these clients have rarely been challenged in their lives. Their self-esteem has been fostered since they were in grade school, and they pretty much have always had their needs met. This does not just have to do with materialistic things such as clothes and cars—although having *every* need satiated is a major contributing factor. What I am talking about is never letting a child face adversity or having to suffer for or work for the things they want.

For instance, instead of blaming a child for poor performance, many parents will instead blame the teacher for being too hard on their son/daughter. Instead of making their child work a part-time job for a car or clothes, luxuries are given to them just because the parents can afford to do so. He's the football player who is bailed out of jail for a DUI because he has a game the next day and it might jeopardize his scholarship. He's the private school student who should have been kicked out of school for poor grades, but is given extra chances so he doesn't have to change schools.

The stories are endless, but the end result is the same. We are all guilty of it—even as clinicians—we can fall for the sad puppy-dog eyes and the promises of "next time will be different." But all of the above factors combine to make a generation of students who not only feel as though they are entitled to everything they want in the world, they expect it be given to them "just because." As soon as they experience any adversity, they fold because their confidence is just a hollow shell, and they really don't have the fortitude to deal with it.

Instead of looking inward and blaming themselves, they lash out at their teachers for being unfair, their parents for being too involved in their lives, the college for not teaching them well enough, and so forth. The excuses are endless. When parents try to set boundaries, the kids simply don't care and go on with their selfish views. They feel they are entitled to the college life and how dare anybody take it away. When mom and dad decide to take it away . . . God help them. Typically, we see narcissists lash out at those who dare try to take away what they are entitled to. For example: Larry was an eighteen-year-old high school senior who had been struggling with substance abuse and poor grade performance. Every week I heard a new story about how Larry would lash out at his mother, and then would run away to his father's house to say how mean his mother was and how she overreacted to everything. After finally getting both parents to realize how Larry was pitting one against the other, I got them to agree to a clear contract with boundaries. After failing his spring classes, we set up a contract to indicate that if he failed his summer courses, he would be pulled out of his expensive private school and be placed in a public school.

Larry argued throughout the spring how important the school was to him and how he needed to be with his friends for his senior year. Not surprisingly, Larry failed his summer classes, and it came time for Larry's parents to stick to the plan. At first his parents wanted to give him one more chance, but I expressed to them how that would only reinforce his view that he could talk his way around anything and would never get the experience of living with the consequences of his poor choices. They agreed to stick to their word and, like clockwork, Larry yelled and screamed at his parents. He said they were being so unfair and that they were teaming up against him. When I reframed the decision, went over the series of events (i.e., failing grades and drug use), asked him how he lived up to his word, and pressed him to explain how his actions could be interpreted as somebody who really wanted to be at that school, he simply answered that "it just wasn't fair and they were wrong."

I share with you this case example because this is where it all begins. Its incidents like this that eventually turn children into the problems that we see today. Narcissism starts early and is fostered by society in general but by parents/families as well.

Now, narcissism is not all about an inflated sense of self which leads to selfish behaviors. Larry Bugen, PhD, author of *Stuck on Me: Missing You*, distinguishes between the grandiose versus morose types of narcissism. The grandiose is the usual type we think of when we conjure up an image of bulging chests, pumping fists, and grandiose life styles filled with prideful boasting and excess. But Bugen also goes on to describe the morose narcissist—the chronically depressed—or individuals obsessed with failure and self-doubts. No matter whether one is grandiose or morose, the interpersonal costs are the same: these individuals live in a world unto themselves, failing to see others, engage others, or empathize with others because of their preoccupation with themselves.

In the case of the morose, some individuals become suicidal—the ultimate selfish act—because the person only thinks about escaping his own pain and does not think about what his action does to everybody around him

He explains that some people will feel so unfairly treated by society, feel as though their needs have never been met, feel so glaringly unhappy that they have earned the right to do what is in their best interests and only look at meeting their own needs. This very dynamic is the reason why we consider suicide the ultimate selfish act—because the person only thinks about escaping his own pain and does not think about what his action does to everybody around him.

In a more relatable sense, how many of you have children who you know are depressed but are acting out in ways that are extremely selfish? Many clients who walk into our clinic will talk about how unhappy they are and how unfair life has been to them—using that rationale as a way to explain why they go out and party every night at school, why they abuse drugs, why they are promiscuous, why it's okay to lash out at their parents. For example: Sally is a twenty-year-old college student who was brought into our clinic for severe problems with anxiety, depression, eating disorders, ADHD, and poor interpersonal relationships. This particular client had an extremely bad relationship with her parents and was always lashing out at them and demanding their respect at the same time.

Sally was failing out of school and was forced to move home because she was kicked out of her dorm for drinking on campus. After moving back home, she continued to berate her parents, and the discord grew to a point where her parents said they were through with her and were ready to disown her. Sally had very little insight into her behavior and blamed her parents for everything. She could not understand why everybody was against her. She believed that she was entitled to do the things she was doing and people just were not giving her the respect that she needed.

After several months of intense therapy, it turned out there was a significant trauma in Sally's past, and she subconsciously hated her parents for not doing enough to stand up for her. It was this seed of hurt, anger, and resentment that fueled her negative self-worth and propelled her narcissistic preoccupation with herself.

To complicate matters even worse is the pressure that society places on children today. When my parents were being raised, there was no Internet and much of the shows on TV were wholesome and made for the whole family to watch. Now, parents get to compete with twenty-four-hour reality television and the Internet. There has never been a time when parents' influence on their children has been lower. Parents can do everything in their power to pass on their values about hard work, sacrifice, faith, and honesty. But unfortunately, television and the Internet might have more power over your children.

While the jury may be out on whether violent video games/movies cause violent behavior in kids (Bushman & Anderson, 2001), it's tough to argue how reality television has profoundly affected our society. How many of us really knew what Coach handbags and Jimmy Choo shoes were before Paris Hilton and the *Real Housewives of Orange County*?

If you look at MTV's ratings, shows like *The Jersey Shore* and *The Hills* are always near the top. If you look at E! and VH1, shows like *Paris Hilton BFF* and *Keeping Up with the Kardashian's* are near the top as well . . . all in the important eighteen to twenty-two age group. What do all of these shows have in common? Give up?

They all revolve around a group of people who do absolutely nothing other than create drama around themselves, and they are engrained in American pop culture as a result. Whether people want to call *The Jersey Shore* a guilty pleasure or mindless entertainment, we need to call the show out for what it is. It showcases people who have done nothing in their lives except party all the time, and they are rich as a result. It is the new American dream and the eighteen- to twenty-two-year-old age group is eating it up. I don't know how many times, in the past month, one of the Kardashian's has been on a talk show, and I still can't figure out why they are famous.

They are young and wealthy and are sending out a message that this is the American dream: do absolutely nothing and become rich and famous. I look at these shows, and I am almost surprised that we wonder why kids are failing to launch all over the place.

But as I sit here and write, I know that there are greater factors at play here that are contributing to this problem. What is kind of interesting is that I feel as though my generation is a bridge generation. What I mean by that is that my generation is a bridge to baby boomers and a bridge to the millennial generation. The millennials are too young to really understand the baby boomers and the baby boomers are too old to really understand the millennials. This puts my generation of clinicians in an interesting spot because I think we can look in to the past and understand why the baby boomers did what they did, but also modern enough to be able to relate to the millennials.

When I look at the millennials, I see a generation that cannot see past their own noses. They have a blind arrogance to them that makes them feel as though they have all of the answers and have a built-in defense to prevent any new insights from changing their internal working models about themselves, others, and their place in the world. While every young generation can be described as arrogant and determined to prove the previous generation wrong, this generation scares me because so much of what they do is based on a lie that they continue to tell themselves. Allow me to digress for a moment to explain myself.

When we look at the baby boomers when they were young adults, they were in the middle of a counterculture movement that was hell-bent on trying to change American society. The baby boomers were raised in the 1950s and 1960s in constant fear of the cold war, communism, nuclear arms, and the Vietnam War. They were tired of being scared about everything and decided that they were not going to listen to their parents' generation (i.e., society, government, etc.) anymore. They decided that what made life worth living was peace, love for one another, and universal understanding of one another. Instead of letting world governments tell us every man for himself and to fear those who were not like us, they wanted to try a new approach where we all look out for each other.

When we look at the Woodstock Concert in 1969, all people gushed about was peace, love, and understanding for one another. People were literally intoxicated with how peaceful everybody was and how five hundred thousand people could co-exist peacefully for a common goal. Their hope was that the concert would send a message to the rest of the world that would create a critical mass of change.

Of course much of the peace, love, and understanding were the by-product of copious amounts of drugs such as marijuana, LSD, among others. While growing up, I heard all of the glory stories about drugs and amazing psychedelic/spiritual experiences that the baby-boomer generation had. With an untrained ear, it is very easy to interpret those stories as advocacy for drug use and getting really stoned . . . but that's not what their stories were about. Their stories were about a generation so desperate to connect with one another and find peace in the world that they turned to psychedelic substances to connect with each other in a deeper way. The drug use was not about escaping from problems or isolating their minds from the world, it was about finding ways to experience each other and the world in a much deeper and meaningful way.

In the 1960s and 1970s, researchers in psychology departments across the United States were experimenting with psychedelics to measure psychic abilities, transpersonal psychology experimentation (Bakalar & Grinspoon, 1990). While mainstream psychology will not readily flaunt these facts, there were many early psychotherapists that would use LSD, marijuana, MDMA, and other hallucinogens to help people through their psychological problems and to relate on a different level of consciousness with the therapist or other people in group therapy sessions.

The baby boomers understood this on a certain level and did not pretend that psychedelics were anything but a tool to expand the mind. However, as the 1970s wore on, the experiment failed and instead of expanding the mind, people became slaves to their own minds as a result of addiction. When soldiers from Vietnam began bringing their heroin habits back home, it quickly spread to the counterculture, and soon the country was struggling with its first major problem with drug addiction. When people in the counterculture began seeing their friends, family, and music icons dying from substance abuse problems, their views about the usefulness of drugs as a tool to bring people together changed dramatically.

The baby boomers slowly assimilated into the American system and they began having children, and the lessons of the counterculture movement were lost, instead to be replaced with glory stories of drug use and Hollywood glorification of raging parties, crazy rock bands, and absurd drug experiences.

Why I am covering all this is because the crutch of the millennials lies in the above narrative of a young baby-boomer generation. While I may be arrogant about my own generation, I truly feel as though we were able to grasp the notion of what it meant to be a baby boomer in the 1960s and 1970s and what their actions were really about. We heard the glory stories, but we didn't mistake it for condoning of a crazy drug- and alcohol-fueled young adult existence, but as a life lesson to learn from. We understood that our parents were not condoning debauchery; they were just trying to get us to realize that you can have peace, love, and understanding when you are strung out on drugs. Yes they had a good time while they were doing it, but we saw it for what it was.

We also understood their message that their hearts were in the right place and they were trying to create a new a better world for their children. Their vision for the future did not pan out, but their message of trying to make the world a better place was not lost on us.

The millennials are too far removed from the baby boomers to begin to even understand what the counterculture movement is all about. Further complicating the millennials is that they are too egocentric to even admit that maybe they have misinterpreted the events of the past and instead have a warped new reality of what life is really about. The millennials have been brainwashed by countless hours of television that condition them to associate getting hammered (a la *Jersey Shore*) to being famous and cool. They have been bombarded with music that corresponds success with having expensive cars, big homes, and getting drunk/stoned all of the time.

What the millennials have internalized is not a message of peace, love, understanding, and making the world a better place. Instead, they have internalized a message of blind decadence, debauchery, self-indulgence, self-serving principles, and vanity. Instead of trying to expand their minds and wanting to connect with one another on a deeper level; they have adopted a schema of avoidance, entitlement, self-gratification, and social Darwinism.

What is almost comical is that they have no insight into their own actions, so they will never have the ability to see their lifestyle for what it really is. They convince themselves that their lifestyle has some other greater meaning and that they are the ones who are actually being misinterpreted by the older generations. In an ironic twist of fate, the millennials conjure up all of the stories about their parents and grandparents using drugs and alcohol to justify their actions, claiming that they are doing the same exact thing as they. But it is not the same thing and we cannot let them fool themselves anymore. This is a generation that is trying to avoid the challenges of life in any way possible.

The truth of that matter is that life can be quite painful. As a person I have experienced much pain in my life and have seen people I love in incredible emotional pain and grief. As a clinician, I have witnessed my clients experiencing the same emotional struggles. All of us can relate to each other's pain because we have all experienced it ourselves. Life is filled with many ups and downs and sometimes the downs really f'ing suck. But . . . pain is part of the human experience.

While pleasure and happiness are powerful and fun emotions, we cannot gorge ourselves on those emotions and just ignore the negative emotions. It is all or nothing when it comes to emotions. We either feel all of them or none of them. This generation is trying to gorge themselves like id driven monsters and use drugs, alcohol, money, and sex to numb out all of the negative emotions and feel awesome all the time. The words of the late Samuel Johnson (1809) perhaps summarized it best: "He who makes a beast of himself rids himself the pain of being a man."

We have the problem of failure to launch because we have sent the wrong message, taught the wrong messages, and allowed society and Hollywood to raise our children for us. Through passivity, we have created this monster ourselves, and it is up to us to finally clean up the mess.

Chapter Three

So Are They Narcissistic, Entitled, or Just a Bunch of A$!hol&s?

When we think about narcissists, we often think of the pompous football player who thanks his hands for being so great when he catches the game-winning touchdown, but will say that his quarterback is garbage and cannot throw when he drops the game-winning catch. When challenged by the player or the team's coach, he stages a locker room coup and lashes out at anybody who lays the blame at his feet. In these cases, the rage the player exhibits serves the purpose to hide his fragile ego state from the masses and to a great extent . . . to hide his fragile ego state from his own consciousness.

One of the reasons many therapists do not work with clients with narcissistic personality disorder is because they do not have any insight into their own behavior. It is very challenging to work with people who do not see themselves in an accurate light and often reject any piece of information that disagrees with their own internal working models. The narcissist must reject any insight because, if they had insight, they would see that their outward overconfident personality is merely a mask that they wear to protect themselves from experiencing their own low self-worth and their fears of rejection from others.

They would see that the turmoil that they cause around them is not the result of incompetent and jealous people, but rather the results of interacting with a person who only cares about themselves, using other people for their own gain, and punishing people who dare challenge their abilities. Because the narcissist does not have the ego strength to handle the truth, they must subconsciously reject any notion of reality.

I often find it amusing, in the beginning stages of treatment, when I am interviewing the parents and the child to gather information about the family system. When I speak to the parents, I get a detailed view of a family system in disarray with numerous stories about how their child is disrespectful, lazy, and often aggressive when challenged. When I get the child's point of view, I get a completely different story that, more so than not, paints the blame with the parents. They have unfair expectations and are actually the ones to blame for the whole problem.

While I can admit that I have worked with my fair share of parents who do not see the situation accurately, the vast majority of the time the child has their own view of reality that is loosely based on facts. In many cases, this child is not flat out lying to me, but rather simply explaining their limited and egocentric view of the family. It is important to remember that the adult child in these family systems simply do not have the insight to see themselves and their actions for what they really are.

When I first began working with this population, I can admit that at first I thought I was working with a bunch of little narcissists and that the next generation was probably screwed. I remember several conversations with my wife about having children and my fear that our kids were going to be assholes. Of course, I may be exaggerating my fears of my children being assholes, but I think this brings up an important discussion about what we are really dealing with here in these clients. In later chapters, I will discuss the importance of diagnosis and assessment in treatment, but I think I need to take a second to clarify my views on whether these clients are truly diagnosable as having narcissistic personality disorder.

The Diagnostic and Statistical Manual for Mental Illness IV (DSM-IV) states the following criteria for narcissistic personality disorder:

A pervasive pattern of grandiosity (in fantasy or behavior), need for admiration, and lack of empathy, beginning by early adulthood and present in a variety of contexts, as indicated by five (or more) of the following:

- Has a grandiose sense of self-importance (e.g., exaggerates achievements and talents, expects to be recognized as superior without commensurate achievements)
- Is preoccupied with fantasies of unlimited success, power, brilliance, beauty, or ideal love
- Believes that he or she is "special" and unique and can only be understood by, or should associate with, other special or high-status people (or institutions)
- Requires excessive admiration
- Has a sense of entitlement, that is, unreasonable expectations of especially favorable treatment or automatic compliance with his or her expectations
- Is interpersonally exploitative, that is, takes advantage of others to achieve his or her own ends

- Lacks empathy: is unwilling to recognize or identify with the feelings and needs of others
- Is often envious of others or believes others are envious of him or her
- Shows arrogant, haughty behaviors or attitudes

I remember reading these criteria to a frustrated parent, and she responded with a laugh and said that her child met every one of these criteria. When I take a look back at the many clients whom I have worked with in these situations, I would say that at any point in time, 80 percent of my clients would fit the criteria for a diagnosis of narcissistic personality disorder. When I speak to clinicians on this topic, I get similar responses from them as well. Either our practices are a magnet for this disorder or there is much more to assess with our clients than just simple criteria.

According to the National Institute on Mental Health, their latest estimates have narcissistic personality disorder affecting 1 percent of the population, which lends credence to the assumption that we cannot simply diagnose every child we see as a full-blown narcissist. This is why we need to look at narcissism on a continuum; with each client displaying varying levels of narcissism.

On one end of the spectrum you have clients who are simply egocentric; meaning that they have a worldview that is centered on themself. Clients who struggle with egocentrism often put more importance on their own experiences rather than the experiences of other people. In Piaget's Theory of Cognitive Development, it is not until the concrete operational stage (ages seven to eleven) that children's thinking becomes less egocentric; meaning that they begin to see themselves from multiple perspectives.

While many of Piaget's theories ring very true, I have not run into many eleven-year-old children who can define their actions through a perspective other than their own. In fact, how many adolescents do we know that we would not define as egocentric? The prefrontal cortex of the human brain plays the biggest role in self-insight, and coincidentally research has shown that this part of the brain does not fully develop until the age of twenty-one in females and twenty-three in males (Fields, 2005). This suggests that egocentrism is neurologically innate in people ages seven to twenty-three and is actually more normal than pathological.

For clients who fall into the egocentric range of narcissism, you will likely see a person who will only define the problem in the family system from their own perspective and will have only considered how the situation in the home has affected them rather than how it has also affected the family. The client usually has some level of insight and typically responds well to honest feedback about their behaviors. While there is some level of insight with clients in this range, they do experience some defensiveness and will show some resistance to looking at their behavior. But overall, these clients have ego strength to deal with life's problems and need some work to learn how to view life and their problems from multiple perspectives.

The next level on this continuum would be what I consider entitled clients. These clients have higher levels of narcissism than an egocentric child, but still do not meet full criteria for narcissistic personality disorder. When looking at these clients, you will commonly see a childhood history of overindulgence. What I mean by overindulgence is a history of parents giving in to their child's demand and desires. Most parents want their children to be happy, but the problem with giving a child everything they want is that they learn to expect that they will always get what they want.

In Freud's view, we have the id, which is our innate desire to satiate every desire that we have. The id wants what it wants, and it wants it now, regardless of what it has to do to get it. As we develop, we develop the ego, which gives the id what it wants, but learns to satiate the id with a certain set of moral codes and with a bit of delayed gratification. Ultimately, we develop the super ego which helps regulate the id and ego and also poses the question of whether we even need to have that need satiated at all.

What happens with a parent who spoils a child is that they are conditioned to be id driven without ever having the experience of learning to delay gratification or put off gratification at all. By the time they reach adolescent age, they are id machines who want what they want and they want it now; because that's what life has been up to this point. When a child doesn't get what they want, they feel as though they are entitled to it and lash out at those who do not give it to them. Due to their lack of insight, they do not see that their request is off base, but rather it is the parents' fault for not giving in to their needs.

In our failure-to-launch clients, college, spending money, cars, credit cards, clothes, and so forth are not something they view as privileges or rewards . . . they are looked at as an entitlements. It is something that they earned as a birthright, and regardless of what they do with it, mom and dad have to give it to them. When they fail their classes, mom and dad have no right to get mad at them. When they wreck their car after coming home drunk, mom and dad can't be mad and have to fix it. I can go on for days on this group. The bottom line is that many of the clients that you see fall in to this category, and the problem is very much a family systems issue as well as an individual issue.

The next group is what I call the self-loathing narcissist. As I touched on in the previous chapter, narcissism is not just an overinflated sense of self, but also in many cases about a total lack of self-esteem. In many of my clients, I will have a client who is profoundly depressed, self-loathing, unmotivated, and completely focused on their subjective experience of the world. These clients will be so focused on their own pain that they will often totally forget that they live in a family who gets to put up with them every single day.

Whether it be the outbursts, failed promises, lies, suicide attempts, drug use, or the wasting of family resources . . . they do not see how their actions are affecting the people who care for them. When I ask a client in this category about how their depression affects their parents, I usually get responses that they never thought about it or that their parents just don't seem to care/understand. In other cases, clients in this category will often blame their parents for the outcome of their life. When I asked a client recently about what his parents should do to help, he responded,

> Well, all they do is bug me to get a job and go to school. If they would just leave me alone maybe I could get a job. I really blame them to be honest. Their nagging just hurts my self-esteem and makes me more depressed. They just need to let me stay here for a few more months so I can regroup and work on myself.

What's interesting in this case is that this client had already been living at home over a year after failing out of college twice and refuses to speak with his parents. When he does respond, it's often with a facetious attitude and curse words. As we see in this type of client, they are so unhappy they feel entitled to doing nothing and blame everybody else for their problems. They are so wounded and broken that they have earned the right to focus on their needs and their needs only. This is why we consider suicide the most selfish act. People who commit suicide are only focused on ending their pain. They do not take a moment to think of how their actions will affect other people.

The last group on this continuum is what I consider diagnosable narcissists. The irony is that maybe 5 percent of my clients really fall in to this group, and even with that 5 percent, they don't fall into the typical presentation of an adult narcissist per se. Typically, with clients in this group, you will most likely see some sort of comorbidity with an addiction. Whether it be drugs, alcohol, or process addiction, these clients will usually struggle with one or more of these addictions.

These clients are extremely difficult to work with because most of them do not see themselves as a problem and have no empathy for how their actions affect the family. Many times you will hear a parent talk about the lies that the client tells them to forgive them, which is usually followed up with another attachment wound such as stealing money, credit card fraud, selling house items, or just manipulating the parent to give them what they want. This is what I call "the setup." I always warn parents for the setup with these clients . . . if it sounds too good to be true, then it typically is.

In my opinion, substance abuse is comorbid with this group because they are typically too young to develop full narcissistic personality traits. At this age it's usually an addiction that accelerates the process. It's the addiction that makes them hurt the people that are close to them, and the families have a difficult time letting go of the idealized or prodigal son image from their brain. The addiction has changed their child, and because getting high or getting their fix is more important to them, they will hurt anybody or use anybody to get high. As I stated earlier, these are very difficult people to work with, and as I will explain in later chapters, much of the work will be with the family system rather than the client.

While the clients that we deal with will fall in to different categories on the narcissism continuum, there is a major common behavior that is evident throughout—narcissistic rage. When parents come in to my office and begin to explain what life is like inside their home with the client, one word they almost always use is that they feel like they are "walking on egg shells" around their child. When asked to explain further, parents explain that whenever they try to engage their child in a conversation about their future, it is always met with anger, curse words, and a clear message to leave them alone.

After enough time has passed, parents also add that even regular conversations with their child are impossible to have with them. When I ask parents how they have dealt with this, I usually get the answer of "We just leave him alone." It is at this point in the family system that the child has taken the power away from the parents and locked the system into a dynamic that prevents any type of change from happening. Take the following case example as an illustration:

Leonard is a twenty-year-old male who lives at home and is clueless as to what his next move in life should be. When he was eighteen years old, Leonard left home for college in a neighboring state and quickly ran into academic problems at school. He admitted that he began smoking marijuana on a daily basis with his roommates and rarely went to his classes. He went on academic probation by his second semester and was eventually kicked out of school by the end of the year. Leonard returned home, his parents got him an apartment, and he worked full-time as a pizza delivery man. Leonard's marijuana use spiraled, and he soon found himself isolating from friends and family, often spending hours in a dark room and playing video games all day. When he got into a car accident while on the job, he was fired from his job and eventually was evicted from the apartment. By this time, Leonard was displaying several symptoms of anxiety and depression, and his parents were concerned for his safety. Leonard moved in with his mother and largely smoked marijuana all day and refused to find a job. Leonard's mother explained that she saw how unhappy he was and let him off the hook for several weeks because she was worried about him and did not want to push him over the edge.

After it became apparent that Leonard was not moving forward, she began to ask him about going back to school and finding a job. Whenever she brought this up, Leonard would lash out at her with intense anger. He would say how miserable he was, how much he hated his life, and how her getting on him to find a job only made him feel worse. He would disappear for several hours, return home extremely stoned and would isolate himself in his room. This cycle continued for several weeks before his mother finally contacted me to help. When she came into my office, she was crying the entire session and said she felt like a prisoner in her own home. She could not talk to her son and felt powerless to make any changes. Furthermore, she was afraid that if she pushed him any further, he might hurt himself.

As you can see in the above case example, the child in this family system was using his rage as a means to scare his mother into not taking any action. This is the beauty of narcissistic rage in these cases; it totally paralyzes the system and keeps things exactly the same way . . . which is exactly what the child wants.

One of the most important things to understand about these types of reactions to confrontation is that narcissistic rage is a defensive reaction. Sigmund Freud, one of the first personality theorists to discuss narcissism and defensive reactions, believed that rage was a defensive reaction to a *narcissistic* perceived threat to a narcissist's self-esteem or self-worth (Kahn, 2002). According to psychodynamic theory, narcissists put up a narcissistic shell to protect themselves from narcissistic injury.

The shell is often portrayed to other people as an overinflated sense of self or as having an overabundance of self-confidence. This shell, however, is fake and can easy be shattered because on the inside is really a vulnerable person with no self-esteem at all. Object relations theory states that the narcissist outer shell serves as a means to coverup the *putrid core* of the person. If the outer layer of the narcissist is broken, people will see the narcissist for who they really are, hence the narcissist with fall apart and not have the ego strength to put themselves back together again.

Since the confidence and arrogance that a narcissist displays is only a shell, it can be broken quite easily when it is challenged. This is why when a narcissist is challenged, they lash out with rage to keep people away from them; to prevent themselves from falling apart and to prevent people from seeing them for who they really are. When a narcissist experiences an intense narcissistic injury, the explosion of rage typically is experienced on two levels. The first being rage aimed at others, and the second layer is aimed at oneself.

I liken this reaction to a fuel-air bomb that the U.S. military uses. It produces such an intense explosion, that it uses up all of the oxygen in the surrounding area and it sucks in oxygen from surrounding areas and implodes on itself. When a narcissist rages, he lashes out intensely at other people whom they perceive as hurting them, then runs out of energy and implodes in on itself and self-loathes.

To begin to change the system, we must address narcissistic rage and attempt to change this dynamic not only with the client, but the parent as well. It is this rage that scares or guilt's a parent into becoming an enabler.

Chapter Four

The Loving Enabler

So what exactly is enabling and how does it play out with our failure-to-launch clients? According to the Merriam-Webster Dictionary, enabling is defined as to supply with the means, opportunity to do something. Moreover, it is also defined as to make practical, possible, or easy. When we look at enabling with a drug addict, we very much see a person within the family system who enables the addict and continues the addiction cycle. Unless the enabler stops their behaviors and puts up better boundaries between him- or herself and the addict, then the system will never change and the addict will continue to use.

We have all seen enough episodes of *Intervention* on Bravo to understand what an enabler looks like in a family system and how to address these issues with a drug-addicted client. Unfortunately for our failure-to-launch children, the symptoms of enabling are not as visible to the people within the family system. Nevertheless, enabling behaviors are a key problem in these families and must be dealt with if we expect any positive changes in our clients.

Let's take a look at the following case example so I can illustrate the role of enabling in a failure-to-launch client: Brian was a twenty-four-year-old client who presented for counseling with his mother. When asked what brought them in for counseling, Brian's mother began by saying that she was frustrated with his lack of initiative and his lack of movement in his life. She explained that Brian failed out of a state university when he was twenty years old and has been living at home ever since. He started community college several times but only would go to classes for a few weeks before quitting because it was too difficult on him. She went on to explain that she was very concerned about his mental well-being when he returned home and thought that getting a job or staying in school might be too stressful for him. Whenever she challenged him to get a job or go back to school, he would have anxiety attacks and would not leave his room for more than a few hours at a time. As time wore on, his depressive symptoms increased and he was paralyzed by his anxiety. As a means to cope with his anxiety, Brian began to smoke marijuana on a regular basis and mostly stayed in his room all day and played video games.

A few weeks prior to presenting for counseling, Brian was challenged to start school again and get a job. Unable to deal with the challenge, Brian admitted himself to a local behavioral health hospital and was diagnosed with borderline personality disorder. When I asked Brian about his experience of the problems, he indicated that he was just very depressed and has no energy or motivation to do anything. Furthermore he stated that he was socially anxious and felt judged by people all of the time and did not want to be confronted or be around other people. When I asked him how he supported himself, he said that his mother did everything for him. He explained that she does his laundry, cooks for him, makes his appointments, wakes him up, cleans up his room, grocery shops for him, and even admitted that she dispenses his marijuana to him so he does not smoke too much.

As therapy with Brian unfolded, he made no progress and did not do a single assignment that I asked him to do. When I challenged Brian about his lack of progress and how I believed he did not want to get any better, he agreed and said that why would he want to do anything when his mom does it all for him. He stated that he knows his mother would not kick him out and despite how unhappy he is with not making any progress in life, it's just easier for him to sit home all day, play games, and smoke pot. He even went so far to say that he knows his mom enables him and said that if she would just force him to do everything, he would do it himself . . . he just chooses not to.

Brian gave me permission to speak with his mother, and I disclosed to her his admissions and instead of shock, she responded with defensiveness and anxiety. She nervously stated that she was worried that if she kicks him out, he will be homeless or will hurt himself and she could not live with that for the rest of her life. When I asked her about letting him do certain things on his own such as cooking his own meals or shopping on his own, she responded with, "What will he do for food, what if he doesn't eat?" When I reframed my fears that he will not make any progress unless he is forced to change (using his exact words), she once again said that she could not kick him out and we would have to discuss other options.

As you can see in the above case example, it was very clear that the mother was as much to blame for the problem with Brian as he was himself. Without the mother making any changes to her behavior, the client himself said that he would never change. When challenged to make some changes, his anxiety increased and she was forced to make an internal decision—do I make the changes necessary and learn to deal with my own anxiety or do I continue with the same behaviors and enable my child? In this case, the client's mother chose to continue the same behaviors and enable her son, thus keeping the family system in disarray.

What's interesting with clients such as this family is that their enabling behaviors are completely out of their awareness. Even when it is clearly laid out to them, they are unable to see how they contribute to their child's problems. While it is very difficult to get an enabler to see their own behavior for what it is, I have found a way of explaining it that seems to have helped immensely. I tell the parent that if we were to substitute video games, sleeping in, being unemployed, and so forth, with cocaine or heroin, then we would be talking about a drug problem and you are enabling their drug problem. When it is explained in those blunt terms, most of the parents "get it" at that point in time and acknowledge to me that they understand and agree.

Think about it for a second here: What really is the difference between the above case examples, mom and an enabling parent of a drug addict? She said herself that she was scared if she kicks him out of the house, then he would be homeless and hurt himself. How many times have you heard a parent of a drug addict say that I would rather he use drugs in my house rather than the streets because he might get hurt out there and die? It really is the same thing isn't?

What I tell my failure-to-launch parents is the same thing I tell my drug addicted families: if we continue the same cycle, I know with 100 percent certainty that nothing will change. However, if you are able to stick to your boundaries and your bottom line, then we might have a 50/50 shot of getting the movement that we all want to see. I will take a 50 percent chance of success over a 0 percent chance of success any day of the week.

So let's take a second to actually look at enabling and discuss what are common enabling behaviors and the root causes of enabling behaviors with parents. The most common enabling behaviors that I have found in my practice are:

- Repeatedly bailing them out of jail, financial problems, other "tight spots" they get themselves into.
- Giving them "one more chance," . . . then another . . . and another.
- Ignoring the problem because they get defensive when you bring it up or your hope that it will magically go away.
- Joining them in the behavior when you know they have a problem with it. For example, drinking, gambling, and so forth.
- Joining them in blaming others for their own feelings, problems, and misfortunes.
- Accepting their justifications, excuses, and rationalizations: "I'm destroying myself with alcohol because I'm depressed."

- Avoiding problems: keeping the peace, believing a lack of conflict will help.
- Doing for them what they should be able to do for themselves.
- Softening or removing the natural consequences of the problem behavior.
- Trying to "fix" them or their problem.
- Repeatedly coming to the "rescue."
- Trying to control them or their problem.

One of my favorite enabling behaviors to discuss with parents is repeatedly bailing them out of trouble. This is perhaps one of the worst enabling behaviors because it prevents their children from actually feeling the consequences of their own actions. If we relate this to operant conditioning: it's negative punishment that reduces the likelihood of a person from repeating the same action or behavior. When a parent removes the punishment or tries to soften the punishment that their child would receive, the child does not get the negative reinforcement and will likely repeat the same behavior or action again.

Let me illustrate this with a case example: Tyler was a seventeen-year-old client that I had been working with for several months with impulse control problems and emotional liability. Tyler had been making good progress in school and at home; as well as her parents doing a good job at maintaining a structured environment at home. One day when I went to the waiting room to get Tyler, her mother was with her, and she had an extremely angry look on her face. She immediately wished to speak with me alone and explained to me that Tyler had received a DUI the night before. While the circumstances were a bit unfair, she nonetheless received a DUI, and her mother had finally had enough.

Her mother expressed a feeling of helplessness because Tyler was about to turn eighteen and she did not know what to do to finally get through to her daughter that she had to make better decisions. Furthermore she was livid that her daughter drove her car drunk and was scared that since the car was in her name, if she would have killed or hurt somebody, it would have come back on them.

When I asked her mother what her initial thoughts were on how to handle this situation, she expressed concern about a felony being on her record and what effect it was going to have on her college and professional career. She stated that she spoke to an attorney today, and he thought he could get her out of it. When asked about my thoughts, I told the mother it was not my job what to do but that getting an attorney and getting her out of the ticket would only remove the negative consequences of her actions and reinforce Tyler's view that the rules did not apply to her and she could do whatever she wants. I added that the only real power that she had over her daughter was to let her feel the full consequences of her actions and hope that this was a serious charge and that it would stop her from making the same mistake again in the future.

The mother thought about it for a second and agreed and decided to let her daughter either pay for her own lawyer or to get a public defender. Furthermore, the mother went the extra mile and took the car out of her name when she turned eighteen and made her take over the payments for the car. When asked why she was doing this by her daughter, she replied that since she was going to abuse her car and put herself in danger, she could do it on her own dime and take on the responsibility herself.

This is an excellent example of a parent being confronted with a decision to continue to enable her daughter and get her out of trouble or to stop the enabling process and allow her daughter to feel the consequences of her own actions. Most parents will not realize this or do this on their own; which is why the onus of pointing this out is on the clinician.

Another big enabling behavior that I point out to parents is giving them "another chance." What parents don't realize is that when they continually draw a line in the sand with their children and they fail to maintain that line, it conditions the child to knowing that mom and dad will never keep to their word. If a child knows that mom and dad are not going to enforce any of their consequences, why would they change their behavior?

For example, if a parent tells a child that if they don't get a job by August 1 they are going to be kicked out of the house; only to have August 1 come and go and they do not do anything to the child when he doesn't have the job. From that point forward, the parents have taken away any power that they have over the child because the child knows that their threats are hollow.

If I had to pick another huge enabling behavior, I would choose avoidance as the next runner-up. So many times when a client is lashing out at their parents and using their narcissistic rage as a means to keep people from changing the system, the parents became scared of "waking the beast" per se and decide to avoid upsetting them at all costs. Many parents describe the experience as walking on egg shells and just avoid talking to them or bringing up any topics that might cause the client to become angry and lash out.

I often describe this in terms of a self-fulfilling prophecy to parents; meaning that out of their fear of not wanting any conflict, they try to avoid it altogether. Which in turn perpetuates the problem and it continues to be an issue. Out of not wanting conflict, they actually end up getting conflict. It is vitally important to let parents know how avoidance is enabling the system and how at some point in time they must regain the power from their child and confront the situation.

When I do case consultations with other clinicians, we often marvel at certain client's parents enabling behaviors and are dumbfounded as to why they do not see their behaviors as problematic. The behaviors seem so obvious to us but to the parent in the family system, they do not have any insight in to their behavior at all. Since the parent has no insight at all, it is logical to believe that their enabling behaviors may have as much to do with their child's problems as it does their own psychological problems.

So why do parents enable? In my experience, there are several reasons why parents will become enablers, but there is one common theme that seems to be present in every parent that are enablers. That reason is they love their child, they are a loving enabler. Now I know that sounds kind of weird when I say that loving a child is a major reason for enabling, but I don't think I could find a more true statement.

One of the biggest reasons a parent will enable is that they love their child so much that they will try to protect their child at all costs. They do not want to see their child in pain, they do not want to see their child fail, and they do not want their child to be put into any danger at all. It is for this reason that they will attempt to do everything in their power to prevent those things from happening.

If their child is out of money, they do not want to see them go without, so they will give them money to help make ends meet. If they crash their car, they don't want to see their child have no transportation, so they will buy them a new car. If their child fails out of college, they will send them to a new college because they want them to succeed. If their child gets in trouble with the law, they don't want to see them in jail, so they hire an attorney to get them out of trouble.

The list goes on and on . . . enabling parents will do everything in their power to prevent them from failing because they love them so much. The problem with their logic is that they try so hard to prevent their children from failing that the child never learns what it feels like to fail and has no idea on how to develop ego strength and pick themselves up again. If mom and dad always are there to soften the fall, then they know that they can never fail because mom and dad will always be there. When parents fall in to the loving enabler trap, the child has no real reason to try and succeed and has every reason to take chances that leave not many other options but to fail. Out of their attempt to love and save their child, they actually end up helping them fail.

Many times, a parent's own anxiety is to blame for this cycle. Family systems research has shown a clear correlation between parents' projection of anxiety and later development of anxiety in their children (Isaacson, 1991). When speaking to many parents, the very thought of kicking their child out of the house makes them have an anxiety attack in my office. They begin to catastrophize about them being homeless and getting mugged on the street that it scares them in to keeping them in the house in order to protect them. For many parents, their child has threatened suicide so many times that they fear that pushing him will put him over the edge and they fear he will take his life.

For other parents, it's the fear that they will become drug addicts and will sink into a life of drug use and crime. Once again, out of fear of what might happen, the loving enabler will decide that stoned, lazy, and jobless on their streets is better than the mean streets of Beverly Hills.

A parent's anxiety is not the only culprit in the loving enabler's psyche. Many parents fall in to the "feeling sorry for their children game." Many patients have an extensive history of psychologists, counselors, and psychiatrists by the time they step in to my office. Most of them have been diagnosed with everything from depression/anxiety to ADHD and learning disabilities. Parents will tell their sob stories about how difficult life has been for their child and how life has been so unfair to them. They often point to the fact that they already have no self-esteem and cannot handle anymore failures in their lives. Furthermore, I have many parents who will blame themselves for not being better parents, not being supportive enough, getting divorced, working too much, etc.

When I discuss setting boundaries with these parents, I often get trepidation and sadness about what effect this will have on their child. They already feel as though their child is going to fail with any new boundaries and fear that it will be the straw that breaks the camel's back. The clients themselves will do an excellent job of reinforcing these beliefs because they will often use their unhappiness and low self-esteem to manipulate their parents into not taking any action. As I discussed in the previous chapter, clients will use their narcissistic rage to make their parents feel even guiltier. Which again will make the parent feel powerless to make any changes; ergo no changes happen in the system.

Another culprit in the loving enabler's belief system is something that I like to call "the hidden potential game." Much like the "feeling sorry for your children game," many parents feel as though their child has tons of potential but they just have not figured out the formula for success. They look at their child as the next Nobel prize winner and feel as though just one more change in the environment will make things click.

Maybe it's picking a new college, changing their counselor, another year of maturity, a new medication, and so forth; a parent will come up with a list of things they could change and just do not want to give up on their child. They often state to me that they feel as though if they give up on their child, they will never reach their potential and they cannot live with themselves. So they do what any loving parent will do; they keep pushing the field goal posts in and month after month, year after year, they get the same results.

When I ask a parent in this situation what they are willing to do to get their child to reach their full potential, I usually get the response "anything." What a parent in this situation needs to understand is that if they truly want their child to reach their full potential, they may have to let the child fail. When I first tell this to parents, they often look at me bewildered about how letting a child fail is a path to success. What I then explain to them is that with a child in these situations, you see that he is not motivated and you try to motivate him for himself. This logic while understandable just never works.

In order for a child in this situation to succeed, they must learn to fail so that the environment will pressure them to make changes in their life. There is nothing like living in a crappy apartment and having all of your work money going to rent and utilities to make a child realize that maybe going to college and having mom and dad help support them is a much more viable option.

The last culprit in the enabling family system has nothing to do with the loving enabler, but rather a diversionary tactic by parents. In Salvador Minuchin's family systems theory (1969), he discusses the different levels of a family system and the role of dysfunction in certain family systems. To quickly review, Minuchin believes that a family system has four levels to it. The first level at the top is the individual subsystem, followed by the spousal subsystem, parental subsystem, and finally the child subsystem. When there are problems at the top of the system, they will always create dysfunction in the lower levels of the system.

In terms of a failure-to-launch child, the dysfunction that the child creates in the system, while on the surface disruptive and problematic, actually diverts attention away from other problems in the system. Minuchin called this process *triangulation*. When an adult child is stuck at home and causing significant problems in the home, it will often divert attention away from the problems that exist within the spousal subsystem. When you have a single parent, the child will often divert attention away from problems within the individual subsystem.

While the parents will be very vocal about wanting to see their child succeed, on some levels they want the dysfunction to continue because with the failure-to-launch problem not present, it will force them to look at their own issues and make then take action. Many parents subconsciously or even consciously do not want to deal with those issues, so they will sabotage the process either with inaction or actions that sabotage the whole plan.

Whether it be the loving enabler or just a traditional enabling family system, enabling is a huge part of the problem and must be addressed before any real progress can be expected. Fixing the enabling in the family system will usually be the most important step in the treatment process, or the lack of progress on this front will be the reason treatment will blow up at the launch pad.

II

Underlying Mental Health Issues

Chapter Five

Mood Disorders and Anxiety

If you just read the first part of my book, you could easily think that I believe the failure-to-launch epidemic could be solely blamed on narcissism, entitlement, and enabling family systems. This could not be farther from the truth. The reality of the epidemic is that maybe half of the problem can be attributed to the above reasons, but there is also a whole other category of reasons for why this problem is happening—those reasons being legitimate mental health issues.

Part of being a good clinician is being a good diagnostician, determining what the underlying causes of a person's problems are, and choosing the right intervention to address them. Think about it like this: if a college student comes in to your office and says that he cannot focus on his work and feels as though he cannot succeed in school . . . what logically do you think is the root cause? If you think he is lazy, then much of your work will be on figuring out how to motivate him and maybe some coaching on how to make his work easier. What if he had ADHD that had gone undiagnosed since he was a young child and he finally reached his limit? Then much of your treatment would be on cognitive skills aimed at improving focus, and you would probably make a referral to a psychiatrist for medications.

Let's look at another example: Say you have a client who comes in who has dropped out of college two times due to poor grades, and now he sits at home on his parents couch and plays video games all day. If you believe that he is lazy and just does not want to do anything, then you will probably just help his parents lay down an ultimatum of improving his effort or he can move out. But what if you discover that this client is actually struggling with intense depression and social anxiety which were actually the root causes of his academic problems and lack of effort at home? Then much of your treatment will be focused on traditional psychotherapeutic techniques and also a possible referral to a psychiatrist if the symptoms are severe enough.

As you can clearly see, depending on what you believe is at the root of the problem will totally change your treatment approach. The following chapters will be dedicated to understanding the most common mental health issues that cause the failure-to-launch epidemic, including getting a deeper understanding of mental health issues, how the brain plays a role, how to properly diagnose, and implications for treatment.

According to the NIMH, the prevalence of mood disorders in children and adolescents ages nine to seventeen years is approximately 6 percent. Only one-third of U.S. teenagers with depressive disorders receive treatment. Seventy percent of children with a single major depressive episode will experience a recurrence within five years. Approximately 20 percent of all patients with bipolar disorder experience their first manic episode during adolescence. More than four thousand youth (ages fifteen to twenty-four) in the United States committed suicide in 1998. These stats show the enormity of mental health problems for youth in the United States.

It is distressing for parents to see their child or adolescent sad, withdrawn, or irritable. Yet episodes of sadness and frustration are common during childhood and adolescence. How, then, can a parent or primary care health professional determine whether a child or adolescent is showing signs of a mood disorder? Mood disorders are disorders characterized by disturbances in mood and include major depressive disorder, dysthymic disorder, and bipolar disorder. Depressed mood falls along a continuum. Brief periods of sadness or irritability in response to disappointment or loss are a normal part of growing up and usually resolve quickly in a supportive environment. But some children and adolescents experience intense or long-lasting sadness or irritability that may interfere with self-esteem, friendships, family life, or school performance. These children or adolescents may be suffering from a depressive disorder. Depressive disorders include dysthymic disorder as well as single and recurring episodes of major depressive disorder.

ANXIETY AND DEPRESSION

The brain is the organ that ultimately experiences anxiety and depression because it is the organ of our personality, and thus controls mood, personality, intelligence, and adaptability. Sometimes the brain is the sole cause of anxiety and depression; sometimes it is simply the organ that experiences the results of too much life stress. In most cases, anxiety and depressive illnesses are the result of a combination of brain vulnerability and life stresses.

As we mature, our brain undergoes a process called encephalization, from the posterior aspect of our brain to the frontal lobes. This process occurs throughout the first two decades of life. That's why we as a society focus on education during these years. We also understand that while the brain is developing, we should not drink alcohol, should not smoke cigarettes, shouldn't marry, shouldn't vote, should limit driving responsibilities, as well as other activities that we deem require both maturity and higher-level processing. There are a number of other age restrictions both state as well as federal. On the other hand, our brain seems to normally decline in our older ages from the front to the back. Hence, poor decision making, childlike behavior, impulsivity, as well as other issues seen in pre-senile dementia.

In our earlier years and later years of life, our brains are the most vulnerable to anxiety and depression as well as other life stresses. The brain is involved in everything that we do. The actual physical functioning of your brain heavily influences how well you get along with others, how you think, how you feel, and how you act. These processes are extremely complicated and hence not only are responsible for when things go right, but also lead to the difficulties and huge variability and phenomenological understanding of what goes wrong. The brain is the most complex and powerful organ on earth. It contains over one hundred billion nerve cells, and each of these cells is connected to other cells through hundreds of thousands of individual connections. Exponentially it is estimated that the brain has more than one quadrillion connections within it. Each part of the brain is vastly interconnected with other parts of the brain. There are five major systems in which these connections have been determined to be involved with behavior, and these interconnections in turn lead to several different types of anxiety and depression.

Anxiety and depression are real illnesses. When left untreated, they often have very serious consequences and are responsible for school and failure to launch, and thus long-term job failure, relationship problems, health problems, and sometimes suicide.

Pure Anxiety

Pure Anxiety results from too much activity in the brain's basal ganglia (BG). This category includes generalized anxiety disorder and phobias. Anxiety is a very inheritable, if not the most inheritable disorder outside of addiction disorder. Children and adolescents who experience anxiety are plagued by feelings of panic, fear, and self-doubt, and suffer the physical feelings of anxiety as well, such as muscle tension, nail biting, headaches, abdominal pain, heart palpitations, shortness of breath, and sore muscles. They also are frequently absent from school, and they experience an overload of tension and emotion. The twelve most common symptoms of pure anxiety are:

- Frequent feelings of nervousness or anxiety
- Panic attacks
- Avoidance of places for fear of having an anxiety attack
- Heightened muscle tension
- Periods of heart pounding, nausea, or dizziness
- Tendency to predict the worst
- Multiple, persistent fears or phobias
- Conflict avoidance
- Excessive fear of being judged or scrutinized by others
- Easily startled or tendency to freeze in anxiety-provoking or intense situations
- Seemingly shy, timid, and easily embarrassed
- Bites fingernails or picks skin

Pure Depression and Mixed Anxiety and Depression

Pure depression comes from excessive activity in the brain's emotional center, the deep limbic system (DLS). These symptoms range from chronic mild sadness (dysthymia) to major depression. Hallmark symptoms include:

- Persistent sad or "empty" mood
- Loss of interest or pleasure in activities that are usually fun, including sex
- Restlessness, irritability, or excessive crying
- Feelings of guilt, worthlessness, helplessness, hopelessness, and pessimism
- Sleeping too much or too little, early-morning awakening
- Appetite and/or weight loss, or overeating and weight gain
- Decreased energy, fatigue, feeling "slowed down"
- Thoughts of death or suicide, or suicide attempts
- Difficulty concentrating, remembering, or making decisions
- Persistent physical symptoms that do not respond to treatment, such as headaches, digestive disorders, and chronic pain
- Persistent negativity or chronic low self-esteem
- Persistent feeling of dissatisfaction or boredom

Mixed anxiety and depression is actually more common than we once realized, given the multiple communications between the basal ganglia and the deep limbic system. Eventually if one experiences continued anxiety, one will at some point in time become depressed, and vice versa. One thing for sure is that when anxiety and depression coexist, the situation is severe;

whichever came first or second, the combination can be more devastating and needs to be treated as soon as possible.

The possible signs for depression in infants, children, and adolescents differ and are on a continuum (see table 5.1).

	Infancy	Early childhood	Middle Childhood	Adolescence
Failure to thrive, speech and motor delays, decrease in interactiveness, poor attachment	X			
Repetitive self-soothing behaviors, withdrawal from social contact	X	X		
Loss of previously learned skills (e.g., self-soothing skills, toilet training)	X	X		
Increase in temper tantrums or irritability		X		
Separation anxiety, phobias, poor self-esteem		X	X	X
Reckless and destructive behavior (e.g., unsafe sexual activity, substance abuse)		X	X	X
Somatic complaints		X	X	X
Irritability or withdrawal			X	X
Poor social and academic functioning			X	X
Hopelessness, boredom, emptiness, loss of interest in activities			X	X

Table 5.1. Signs of Depression in Infants, Children, and Adolescents.

Another type of anxiety/depression results from too much or too little activity in the brain's temporal lobes, in addition to too much activity in the BG and/or DLS. When there are problems in this part of the brain, people struggle with temper outbursts, memory problems, mood instability, visual or auditory illusions, and dark, frightening, or evil thoughts. These symptoms are also frequently seen in bipolar disorder; however, this is treated with different medications than from the cyclic anxiety/depression.

Temporal lobe anxiety/depression may be aggravated by the use of serotonergic antidepressants. Indeed we are very aware of the warnings that selective serotonin reuptake inhibitors (SSRIs) come with, the possible increased risk of suicidal ideation and increased aggression. This is where single photon emission computed tomography (SPECT) scans are perhaps significantly useful. Missing this diagnosis and treating someone with an SSRI can lead to a significant decline in functioning and perhaps death. Patients with temporal lobe abnormalities and certain patients who have cyclic mood disorders are the ones at greatest risk.

The temporal lobes are also important in other disorders. People with problems in the temporal lobe also misinterpret comments as negative when they are not, have trouble reading social situations, and appear to have mild paranoia. They may also have episodes of panic or fear for no specific reason, and be preoccupied with religious thoughts. In addition, people with problems in the temporal lobe are the most likely to exhibit aggressive behaviors toward others or themselves.

When the temporal lobes become less active with concentration SPECT scans, these individuals struggle with learning problems. When the temporal lobes are less active on the left side, there is a tendency toward reading problems and irritability; when they are less active on the right side there is a tendency to have trouble reading social situations. These distinguishing characteristics on the SPECT scans help us to determine many etiological characteristics of people who have learning differences, spectrum disorders, and others who have had head concussions. The temporal and frontal lobes are very susceptible to head trauma, as we will see later. Symptoms of this type include at least four items from the pure anxiety and/or pure depression, plus at least four of the following:

- Short fuse or periods of extreme irritability
- Periods of rage with little provocation
- Often misinterprets comments as negative when they are not
- Periods of spaciness or confusion
- Periods of panic and/or fear for no specific reason
- Visual or auditory changes, such as seeing shadows or hearing muffled sounds
- Frequent periods of déjà vu
- Sensitivity or mild paranoia
- Headaches or abdominal pain of uncertain origin
- History of a head injury or family history of violence or explosiveness
- Dark thoughts that may involve suicidal or homicidal thoughts
- Periods of forgetfulness or memory problems

Overfocused Anxiety/Depression

The anterior cingulate gyrus (ACG) is the brain's gear shifter. It allows you to shift your attention from thing to thing, to move from idea to idea, and to see the options in your life. In essence it is responsible for cognitive flexibility. When there are problems in the ACG, usually caused by a lack of the neurotransmitter serotonin, people become unable to shift their attention and become rigid, overfocused, and cognitively inflexible.

Overfocused anxiety/depression results from excessive activity in the brain's ACG, the BG, and/or the DLS. When increased activity in the ACG is combined with excessive BG activity, people get stuck on anxious thoughts. When this is combined with excessive DLS activity, people get stuck on negative, depressing thoughts. Many people get stuck on both anxiety-provoking and depressive thoughts. Obsessive-compulsive disorder (OCD), phobias, eating disorders, and posttraumatic stress disorder (PTSD) fit into this type. This type is also associated with people who worry, tend to hold grudges, and have problems with oppositional or argumentative behavior.

Symptoms include at least four items from the pure anxiety and/or pure depression, plus at least four of the following:

- Excessive or senseless worrying
- Upset when things are out of place or don't go the way you planned
- Tendency to be oppositional or argumentative
- Tendency to have repetitive negative or anxious thoughts
- Tendency toward compulsive or addictive behaviors
- Intense dislike of change
- Tendency to hold grudges
- Difficulty seeing options in situations
- Tendency to hold on to own opinion and not listen to others
- Need to have things done a certain way or you become very upset
- Others complain that you worry too much
- Tend to say no without first thinking about the question

Cyclic Mood Disorders

Another type of mood disorder that can present in childhood or adolescence is bipolar disorder. Although bipolar disorder has been considered uncommon in prepubescent children, evidence suggests that it may not be as rare as previously thought, and that it is often difficult to distinguish from severe forms of attention deficit hyperactivity disorder (ADHD). A child or adolescent who presents with recurrent depressive symptoms, persistently irritable or agitated/hyperactive behaviors, markedly labile mood, reckless or aggressive behaviors, or psychotic symptoms may be experiencing the initial symptoms of a bipolar disorder.

Cyclic anxiety/depression results from excessive focal activity in the brain's BG and/or DLS. In this case these focal areas in the brain act like emotional seizures as the emotional centers hijack the brain for periods of time. Cyclic disorders, such as bipolar disorder, cyclothymia, and premenstrual dysphoric disorder (PMDD), along with panic attacks, fit in this category because they are episodic and unpredictable. In addition in bipolar disorder, when a person is in a manic phase of a bipolar illness, there is increased focal deep limbic activity and patchy increased uptake throughout the brain. The hallmark of this type is a cyclic pattern of anxiety and/or depression.

Symptoms of this type include at least four items from the pure anxiety and/or pure depression, plus at least four of the following:

- Periods of abnormally elevated, depressed, or anxious mood
- Periods of decreased need for sleep, feeling energetic on dramatically less sleep than usual

- Periods of grandiose notions, ideas, or plans
- Periods of increased talking or pressured speech
- Periods of too many thoughts racing through the mind
- Periods of markedly increased energy
- Periods of poor judgment that lead to risk-taking behavior
- Periods of inappropriate social behavior
- Periods of irritability or aggression
- Periods of delusional or psychotic thinking

Treatment

When we look at mood disorders and anxiety, we see that it is legitimately a problem that originates within the brain. When our clients are showing symptoms of depression, anxiety, and so forth, it is vital that we understand why this is happening. If the symptoms that we are seeing are truly neurologically based, then we have to choose interventions that will actually address those problems.

But not all of these problems will be neurologically based. Sometimes external factors such as school stress, relational problems, familial problems, social difficulties, and so forth can cause a client to experience problems with depression and anxiety. Think about it, if you have a death in the family, you will likely experience sadness and grief. It is not the result of a neurochemical imbalance but rather the result of a person going through the grieving process. Since it is not neurologically based, medications are not necessary. The treatment will be more focused on therapeutic interventions.

When we are looking at our failure-to-launch clients, it is imperative that we truly understand whether the outward mood disorder and anxiety symptoms are neurologically based or environmentally based. In many cases it will likely be interplay of both factors. Our job as clinicians is to figure out if therapeutic interventions will help alleviate the symptoms or whether it would be more effective to make a referral to a psychiatrist for medication management.

Since many of my clients are hesitant to take medications, I generally try therapeutic interventions first as well as holistic interventions such as diet, exercise, more regulated sleep, and natural supplements. Natural supplements such as 5-HTP, St. John's wort, and GABA are great natural supplements to recommend to clients who struggle with mood disorders and anxiety. 5-HTP is great for increasing dopamine levels in the brain, while St. John's Wart is great for increasing serotonin levels in the emotion centers of the brain. GABA, which stands for gamma aminobutyric acid, does a great job of down-regulating the parts of the brain involved in anxiety.

A good rule of thumb to consider is if after the client has improved their diet, exercises regularly, sleeps well, takes natural supplements, and is still experiencing high levels of depression and anxiety; then it is a good time to refer to a psychiatrist for medication management. My line of thinking is if after trying everything above and they still experience significant symptoms of depression and anxiety, then it is apparent that the symptoms they are experiencing are neurologically based.

The only time that I will recommend medication management in the beginning is if their depression levels are so severe that it prevents them from functioning normally in life and/or they are experiencing suicidal ideations. Furthermore, if a client is experiencing severe anxiety that is causing anxiety/panic attacks, I will make a referral to a psychiatrist.

Chapter Six

Attention Deficit Hyperactivity Disorder

ADHD results from too little activity in the brain's prefrontal cortex (PFC), in addition to excessive activity in the BG and/or DLS. The PFC is the chief executive officer of the brain. It is responsible for functions such as attention span, forethought, impulse control, organization, motivation, and planning. This type is often seen in conjunction with attention deficit disorder (ADD) or attention deficit hyperactivity disorder (ADHD).

ADHD is a developmental disorder that starts in childhood and is associated with long-standing issues of short attention span, distractibility, disorganization, restlessness, and impulsivity. We believe that ADHD is perhaps one of the more misunderstood mental health problems. There are many myths and common misperceptions that are expressed to us in our practice.

ADHD MYTHS

Myth no. 1: ADHD is the designer disease of the new century.

- ADHD described for over one hundred years
- Stimulants used for ADHD since 1937
- Ritalin introduced in 1951
- ADHD is increasing in the population

Myth no. 2: ADHD is caused by bad parents and teachers.
Myth no. 3: ADHD is overdiagnosed/underdiagnosed.

- Estimated 6 to 10 percent ADHD or ADD

Myth no. 4: People with ADHD just need to try harder.
Myth no. 5: ADHD is only a "minor" disorder.

- Use twice as many medical services
- 35 percent never finish high school
- 43 percent unRx, agg. ADHD boys arrested
- Up to 50 percent of prison population with ADHD or LD
- 52 percent of ADHD adults abuse substances
- 75 percent with interpersonal problems

Myth no. 6: Everybody outgrows ADHD.

- At least 50 percent of children with ADHD have symptoms into adulthood
- Many have never been diagnosed
- For many, leads to serious problems and misdiagnoses

Myth no. 7: ADHD is one disorder.

- With scanning we see different patterns that often present differently and require different treatments

As you can see, when you really look at all of the common myths associated with ADHD, there is not much evidence that supports those myths.

SIGNS AND SYMPTOMS OF ADHD

While we tend to treat our clients on an individual basis including clients with ADHD, there are some common symptoms of ADHD that are present in a majority of our clients who have been diagnosed with the disorder.

Criteria Common to All Types of ADHD

- Short attention span for routine tasks
- Distractibility
- Organizational problems (space and time)
- Difficulty with follow-through
- Poor internal supervision
- Short attention span
- For regular, routine, everyday tasks
- Usually say, "I can pay attention if I'm interested."
- Need adrenaline-filled subjects to pay attention
- Others say they don't seem to listen

Distractibility

- Tend to hear, smell, see, feel, and taste more than others
- Hypersensitive to environmental stimuli
- Poor prefrontal cortex activity cannot inhibit sensory cortex
- Need clothes, food, room, and so forth just right in order to feel comfortable and focus

Disorganization

- Time—frequently late, takes longer than predicted to do projects
- Space—desk, book bag, room, files
- Projects—haphazard approach

Poor Follow-Through

- Multiple interests
- Will do a project only as long as there is intense interest
- May do many things 50 to 80 percent done then stop
- Often gets distracted by other things

Poor Internal Supervision

- Problems with long-term goals
- The moment is what matters
- Takes a crisis-management approach to life
- Problems thinking before words or actions

ADHD THROUGHOUT THE LIFE SPAN

While ADHD is commonly associated with young children, adolescents, and college students, ADHD affects clients of all ages and presents differently throughout the life span. Let's take a look at how ADHD presents and develops throughout the life span.

First Twelve Years—ADHD

- Colicky babies
- Hyperactive/sensitive
- Often unrecognized in girls
- Symptoms include short attention span, distractibility, poor handwriting, poor organization, interrupts frequently, underachievement
- Sleep problems/bedwetting

Adolescence—ADHD

- Often unrecognized, hyperness outgrown
- Presents with impulse control disorders or school underachievement
- Symptoms include short attention span, distractibility, poor handwriting, poor organization, interrupts frequently, underachievement
- Sleep problems
- School failure, often leads to depression
- Impulse control problems
- Teen pregnancy
- Substance abuse
- Runaways
- Legal problems
- Wrong crowd
- Driving problems

Adults—ADHD

- Job failure/changes
- Multiple relationships
- Moves
- Impulse control problems
- Driving issues
- Excitement seeking
- Sleep problems

CAUSES OF ADHD

There are many different theories and research studies that have attempted to identify the underlying causes of ADHD. Here is a sampling of some of those theories:

- Genetics (i.e., being genetically pre-dispositioned for ADHD)
- Brain trauma, especially left frontal lobe
- Prenatal toxic exposure
- Oxygen deprivation
- Brain infections
- Head trauma induced ADHD
- External factors and brain plasticity (i.e., the interplay of social, behavioral, and environmental factors on the brain)

TYPES OF ADHD

While the DSM-*IV TR* only identifies three types of ADHD (primarily inattentive, primarily hyperactive, combined type), Dr. Daniel Amen in *Healing ADD: The Six Different Types of ADD* (2002), utilized SPECT brain imaging to identify six different types of ADHD. Amen explains that it is vitally important to understand what brain structures are involved because different types of ADHD call for different treatments.

This is vitally important to understand with our failure-to-launch clients because many have been diagnosed with ADHD in the past and many have had negative experiences with medications/treatments, so they have not had any treatment for their problems. Many had their symptoms exacerbated by being given the wrong medications or treatment options. When a client is given the wrong treatment, they never get improvement with their symptoms and in fact become hesitant to try any further treatment. Some clients as a result of their troubles express sadness and low self-confidence that they will ever get over their problems (e.g., "I will never be able to pass college").

What Is SPECT Technology?

SPECT stands for single photon emission computed tomography. It is an easy-to-understand imaging technique that looks at areas of the brain that work well, the parts of the brain that do not work hard enough, and the parts of the brain that work too hard.

Six ADHD Types

- Classic ADHD
- Inattentive ADHD
- Overfocused ADHD
- Limbic ADHD
- Temporal lobe AHDD
- Ring of fire ADHD

Type 1: Classic ADHD

- Short attention span (routine matters)
- Distractibility
- Disorganization
- Poor follow-through
- Poor internal supervision
- Restlessness, hyperactivity
- Constant motion, trouble sitting still

- Talkativeness
- Impulsivity
- Lack of forward thinking

Treatment

- Psychostimulants
- Dopamine enhancing supplements
- Higher protein, lower carbohydrate diet
- Intense aerobic exercise
- Neurofeedback
- Very structured environment
- Treat sleep issues

Type 2: Inattentive ADHD

- Short attention span (routine matters)
- Distractibility
- Disorganization
- Poor follow-through
- Poor internal supervision
- Takes a long time to finish tasks
- Daydreams/spacey
- Seems internally preoccupied
- Sluggish
- Low motivation

Type 3: Overfocused ADHD

- Trouble shifting attention, looks like cannot pay attention
- Worrier
- Tends to hold grudges
- Gets stuck on thought patterns
- Can get stuck in patterns of behavior (ritualistic behavior)
- Upset if things do not go your way
- Often argumentative or oppositional
- Trouble shifting
- Often diagnosed with oppositional disorder

Type 4: Temporal Lobe ADHD

- Frequent headaches
- Too sensitive to others

- External aggression
- Dyslexia
- Learning struggles
- Temporal Lobe ADHD
- Aggression

Type 5: Limbic ADHD

- Inattentive (doesn't try)
- Sad, moody, irritable
- Many negative thoughts (ANTs)
- Low motivation, finds little pleasure
- Sleep/appetite problems
- Social isolation

Type 6: Ring of fire

- May be a bipolar equivalent
- Easily distracted
- Too many thoughts
- Often very hyper
- Hyperverbal
- Oppositional
- Aggressive
- Hypersensitive to light, sound, taste, touch
- Moodiness
- Cyclic behavioral changes

Type 6 Ring of fire ADHD treatment

- Anticonvulsants
- New, novel antipsychotic meds
- May also need a stimulant (use last)
- Neurolink

EFFECTIVELY TREATING ADHD

To effective treat ADHD, we need to take a holistic approach to treatment, incorporating multiple modalities to truly alleviate symptoms. Here is a list of common treatment options that we look at with our clients:

- Psycho-education
- Family and professional support

- Medications
- Natural supplements
- Lifestyle changes (diet, exercise, limiting video games)
- Parent training
- School interventions

Treatment Issues

Despite our best attempts to create a holistic treatment approach with our clients, we still run into several problems or experience resistance from the clients and/or their families. Here is a list of common problems that we run into:

- Check perception (i.e., "I will just pay you to solve the problem for me,")
- Magic pill mentality (i.e., "Can't I just take a pill to make it all go away?")
- "Pills no skills" attitude (i.e. "You mean I actually have to work to get better at this?")
- Watch for changes when meds wear off

Supplement Strategies

- PFC—L-tyrosine, 500–1500 mg TID
- AC—St. John's wort 300 mg TID, 5-HTP 100mg TID
- Limbic—DL phenylalanine, 400 mg TID, SAMe, 200–800 mg BID
- Temporal—GABA 100–500 mg BID-TID
- Cyclic—omega-3-fatty acids

Lifestyle Changes

- Head injuries matter—wear helmets, no soccer headers, golf not football
- Avoid toxic substances—alcohol, drugs, nicotine, much caffeine, many medications
- Get enough sleep—less than seven hours decreases brain blood flow
- Manage stress—stress hurts memory centers
- Exercise—boosts blood flow to the brain
- Limit video games—depletes dopamine

Five Steps When Treatment Not Working

- Get a clearer diagnosis
- Balance medication
- Check on interfering factors
- Better follow-through

- Stop cutting corners

With effective holistic treatment of ADHD, it is a highly treatable disorder that can make a dramatic difference in the lives of clients. While some families may be hesitant to invest the time/money in treatment, we have seen the positive effects of treatment with our clients. If we can get movement with our client's symptoms, it can help save money in college tuition, raise self-esteem, create a new career path, and even prevent future generations in the family from struggling with similar problems.

Chapter Seven

Pervasive Developmental Disorders

Pervasive Developmental Disorders (PDD) is a heterogeneous collection of disorders affecting young children's social interaction and ability to communicate, commonly combined with stereotyped behavioral patterns (see table 7.1).

There are two Classifications for PDD:	
DSM-IV	ICD-10
a) Autistic disorder	a) Childhood Autism
b) Rett's disorder	b) Atypical Autism
c) Childhood disintegrative disorder	c) Childhood disintegrative
d) Asperger's disorder	d) Asperger's disorder
e) PDD NOS	e) Overactive disorder with mental retardation & stereotypic movement
	f) Other PDD
	g) PDD unspecified

Table 7.1. Two Classifications for PDD.

When we look at the psychological reasons behind the failure-to-launch epidemic, PDD or more specifically Asperger's syndrome is one of the most prevalent underlying conditions that I am seeing. The DSM-IV TR lists the following criteria for Asperger's syndrome:

1. Qualitative impairment in social interaction, as manifested by at least two of the following:

- Marked impairments in the use of multiple nonverbal behaviors such as eye-to-eye gaze, facial expression, body posture, and gestures to regulate social interaction
- Failure to develop peer relationships appropriate to developmental level
- A lack of spontaneous seeking to share enjoyment, interest, or achievements with other people (e.g., by a lack of showing, bringing, or pointing out objects of interest to other people)
- Lack of social or emotional reciprocity

2. Restricted repetitive and stereotyped patterns of behavior, interests, and activities, as manifested by at least one of the following:

- Encompassing preoccupation with one or more stereotyped and restricted patterns of interest that is abnormal either in intensity or focus
- Apparently inflexible adherence to specific, nonfunctional routines or rituals
- Stereotyped and repetitive motor mannerisms (e.g., hand or finger flapping or twisting, or complex whole-body movements)
- Persistent preoccupation with parts of objects

3. The disturbance causes clinically significant impairments in social, occupational, or other important areas of functioning.
4. There is no clinically significant general delay in language (e.g., single words used by age two years, communicative phrases used by age three years)
5. There is no clinically significant delay in cognitive development or in the development of age-appropriate self-help skills, adaptive behavior (other than in social interaction), and curiosity about the environment in childhood.
6. Criteria are not met for another specific pervasive developmental disorder or schizophrenia.

When you read these criteria, it is difficult to visualize exactly what a client with Asperger's syndrome will really look like. The truth of the matter is that if you have never worked with a client with Asperger's syndrome, then it is difficult to know how to diagnose it. The difficulty with this population is that if you took one hundred clients with Asperger's syndrome, you would have one hundred different presentations and clinical symptoms. Some clients will express mild symptoms, while others may present with more severe problems that affect daily functioning more than others. Many of their symptoms can easily be confused with other disorders such as ADHD, social anxiety, or in layman's terms . . . just weird people.

I have had so many clients come in to my office with a failure-to-launch problem and when I begin to do a developmental history and start gathering clinical information/impressions, it becomes apparent within the first fifteen minutes that this client has Asperger's syndrome. When I ask parents if anybody has ever suggested Asperger's syndrome, they mainly say no and actually do not have a clue what it is.

I am amazed at how many clients will fall through the cracks without ever being diagnosed with this. The signs and symptoms have been there the entire time but nobody thought twice about it. I will usually hear a history of poor social interactions, not having many friends, showing little interest in friendships, black and white thinking, fixation on computers, OCD-like symptoms, inattention, distractibility, hyperfocus, poor problem solving, and a lack of motivation.

Parents usually indicate that they were always concerned about those problems but that he or she did well in high school and just figured he or she was "a little odd" and who were they to judge their child for being weird. The problem continues to progress, and when they fail out of college, they are unable to hold down a job, have no direction in life, have no friends, isolate themselves in their rooms, play video games all day, and so forth; that is when parents finally realize that they need some help and come in to my office.

The sad thing is that all of the research shows that early intervention with Asperger's and autism shows the most promise. When a child is not diagnosed until they are a young adult, our treatment options are limited. The positive news, though, is that more attention has been on autism and Asperger's, and there is more research than ever looking for the underlying causes of it and seeing what new treatments can be developed based on those findings. Let's take a look at some of the research that has been done on Asperger's and what theories have been developed as a result of that research.

Autismus (Latin)–Eugen Bleuler. He derived it from the Greek word autós (αὐτός, meaning self), and used it to mean morbid self-admiration, referring to "autistic withdrawal of the patient to his fantasies, against which any influence from outside becomes an intolerable disturbance."

Dr. Leo Kanner (1943), psychiatrist of the Johns Hopkins Hospital in Baltimore, reported on eleven child patients with striking behavioral similarities, and introduced the label early infantile autism:

- Autistic disturbance of affective contact
- Congenital inability to relate with people
- Not associated with mental retardation

- Described occasional areas of ability splinter skills and uneven and unusual ability called savant skills
- Michael Rutter described autism as a disorder in DSM-III.

At the same time, an Austrian scientist, Dr. Hans Asperger, made similar observations, although his name has since become attached to a different "higher-functioning" form of autism known as Asperger's syndrome.

The prevalence of autism is eight in ten thousand. The ratio of male to female is 4–5:1. Girls with autistic disorder are more likely to have more severe mental retardation. Since autism is associated with higher rates of associated MR and seizures, the biological factors play a strong role. Approximately 75 percent of children with autism have mental retardation (MR):

- One third have mild to moderate MR.
- One half have severe to profound MR.
- 4–32 percent have seizures at some time of their age.
- 20–25 percent show ventricular enlargement (CT Finding).

Genetic factors

- First degree relatives eighty-fold increase
- MZT 60 percent concordance for autism
- 90 percent for broader phenotype
- Chromosomes most common: 2, 7 others 4, 15, and 19
- Genes: Neuroligin, shank 3, contactin associated protein 2, and neurexin 1 (synapse formation)
- ENGRAILED 2 gene for cerebellar patterning is abnormal causing deficit in purkinje neurons
- cMET gene for tangential migration of GABA interneuron leading to imbalance in excitatory and inhibitory neurotransmission
- Reelin gene mutation causing inverted laying of cerebral cortex

Underlying Causes of Gene Abnormality

- Polymorphism
- CNV
- Epigenetics
- Association with genetic disorders like fragile X, tuberculosis, phenylketoneuria, and neuro fibramatosis supports the genetic basis
- Neurodevelopmental basis
- Normal head size at birth with increase in head size at one year
- Abnormal neuro development as indicated by

1. Increase neuro genesis
2. Abnormal migration
3. Decreased neuronal cell death Bcl 2
4. Abnormal synapse formation, pruning

Post-mortem Studies and Neuro Imaging Post Mortem Studies

- Increased brain volumes
- Reduction in purkinje and granule cells of vermis of cerebellum
- Lack of gliosis indicating scaring (suggestive of prenatal origin)
- Reduced neuronal size
- Decreased dendritic arborization
- Increased neuronal packing density in amygdala and hippocampus

MRI

- Increased brain size (temporal parietal occipital)
- Enlarged amygdala and ACG
- Abnormalities of amygdalocortical loopes
- Reduced midsagittal area of vermis
- Reduced purkinji cells but enlarged cerebellum

fMRI

- Abnormal activation
- Amygdala
- Medial prefrontal cortex
- Orbital PFC
- Fusiform gyrus
- Superior temporal sulcus

PET Scan

- Reduced coordinated bran activity

SPECT Scan

- Increased ACG
- Decreased medical prefrontal cortex
- Decreased orbital PFC
- Reduced activity midsagittal area of vermis

The conclusion of these studies is that there is a lack of central coherence of information due to less neural integration and there is increase in brain size at the expense of interconnectivity between neural systems cause fragmented processing.

THEORY OF MIND

Theory of mind (ToM), sometimes used interchangeably with other terms such as mentalizing capacity, is the ability to represent one's own or another's mental states such as intentions, beliefs, wants, desires, and knowledge. This ability is acquired by children around seven years of age and continues to develop until around eleven years of age.

The neurobiological substrate subserving the ability to attribute mental states to oneself and to others is comprised of three main components: posterior regions which include the inferior parietal lobule (IPL) and superior temporal sulcus (STS); limbic-paralimbic regions which include the amygdala, orbitofrontal cortex (OFC), the ventral medial prefrontal cortex (VMPFC), and the anterior cingulate gryus (ACG); and prefrontal regions which include the dorsal medial prefrontal cortex (DMPFC) and the inferolateral frontal cortex (ILFC). There exist reciprocal connections among the regions, which allows for feedback and recursion in processing.

The brain is very fascinating, and when it works well, it's phenomenal, when one of the above pathways misfires or slightly is disrupted for one reason or another, roll a dice. The phenomenological expression of mental disease states very diverse and vast, hence spectrum disorders. The conceptualization deficit view in the ToM is ascribed to individuals with autism, while the application deficit view is generally ascribed to individuals with Asperger's syndrome and the negative symptoms of schizophrenia. The sense of self comes from the right inferior parietal lobule, and the sense of others comes from the STS, Temporal pole, MPFC, OFC, and the amygdala. Mirror neurons found in frontal lobe and STS understands mental state of others.

TREATMENT

As little as ten years ago, the treatment options for autism and Asperger's syndrome were limited. With the research that has been done, we have been able to understand that these disorders are caused by genetic factors and dysfunction in certain parts of the brain. With this data, doctors have been able to develop pharmacological interventions as well as help use this data to shape better behavioral and cognitive interventions.

We have to remember that we have come such a long way in the treatment of autism and Asperger's syndrome. In the 1950s and 1960s, doctors believed that these disorders were caused by bad parenting, and much of treatment was focused helping parents bond to their children more. Current treatments for these disorders focus on medications that help address the neurological issues as well as finding new cognitive and behavioral interventions to improve functioning.

Unfortunately, there is no specific cure or treatment for autism and Asperger's syndrome, so interventions are more focused on reducing specific symptoms that are causing problems in functioning. For example, emotional lability tends to be a significant symptom with clients with Asperger's, so psychiatrists will often prescribe mood stabilizers to regulate the client's mood while psychological interventions focus on emotion regulation skills. If we are trying to treat the excessive rumination/anxiety with these clients, a psychiatrist will usually prescribe an SSRI anti-depressant and a therapist will work on cognitive behavioral techniques such as mindfulness, thought stopping, and so forth.

We have to treat the individual symptoms that are getting in the way of a client's progress. I typically work in conjunction with a psychiatrist to treat the neurological symptoms and then work on specific skills that are aimed at helping improve social skills, emotion regulation skills, independent living skills, interviewing skills, and life coaching. Clients with Asperger's need all the help that they can get. In some cases, however, the symptoms are far too severe and may prevent the client from being able to function independently as an adult. I will discuss how to treat this in later chapters.

Chapter Eight

Substance Abuse

One of the most difficult failure-to-launch populations to work with are clients who struggle with substance abuse. I would say that over 50 percent of the clients that struggle with failure to launch have some type of substance abuse problem. According to a study conducted by the U.S. Health and Human Services Department in 2010, over 21.5 percent of adults aged twenty-one to twenty-five have used illicit drugs. The trends show that number rising every year since 2008.

What we have to understand is that drug use is a significant problem, and we have to account for this with our failure-to-launch clients. The thing that remains unexplained is whether it's the chicken or the egg argument when it comes to drug use and failure to launch. Did the drug use lead to the failure-to-launch problem or did the failure-to-launch problem cause the drug use? We can even argue whether or not drug use just makes the problem worse.

Regardless of how substance abuse interacts with failure to launch, we have to understand how certain drugs affect the brain and in turn how that can affect our failure-to-launch clients. With modern functional brain imaging, we have been able to pinpoint exactly how drugs affect the brain and specifically which parts of the brain are affected.

Each drug has different active ingredients that act on different parts of the brain. The following sections will go over the most commonly abused drugs and see how they act on the brain and the negative impacts that they cause.

SIX DIFFERENT BRAIN TYPES ASSOCIATED WITH ADDICTION

Treating addictions, both process addictions as well as substance abuse/addiction can be very complicated, especially when there are other processes going on. There are some general common brain pathologies that may lead to some understanding in both treatment and understanding of the addicted brain.

There are six different types of brain dysfunction of people who suffer from addiction. I will discuss both the research behind this, the treatments specific to each brain type, as well as other morphological characteristics of each dysfunction.

1. Compulsive: Constant thoughts about addictive substance and/or behavior

- Active anterior cingulate gyrus (ACG) associated with:

Addictions
Eating disorders
OCD
Anxiety disorders
PTSD
PMS
Chronic pain
Oppositional defiant disorder

Increased activity anterior cingulate gyrus and prefrontal cortex is often associated with problems shifting attention which may be clinically manifested by cognitive inflexibility, obsessive thoughts, compulsive behaviors, excessive worrying, argumentativeness, oppositional behavior, or "getting stuck" on certain thoughts or actions. We have seen a strong association with this finding and obsessive-compulsive disorders, oppositional defiant disorders, eating disorders, addictive disorders, anxiety disorders, Tourette's syndrome, and chronic pain (especially when combined with increased basal ganglia activity). If clinically indicated, hyperactivity in this part of the brain may be helped by treatments that increase serotonin.

2. Impulsive: Little control and/or poor judgment about addictive substance and/or addictive behavior

- Low activity in prefrontal cortex (PFC) associated with:

Addictions
ADHD
Depression
Brain trauma
Dementia
Conduct disorders
Antisocial personality
Schizophrenia

Borderline personality

Decreased perfusion in the PFC during a concentration task is often associated with impulsivity, short attention span, distractibility, and difficulties with organization and planning.

3. Impulsive-compulsive: A combination of both of the above types

- Active anterior cingulate gyrus (ACG)
- Low prefrontal cortex activity (PFC)
- See above types.

4. "Sad": Using addictive substance and/or addictive behavior as a way to self-medicate for feelings of sadness, depression, or pain

- Active thalamus
- Addictions
- Mood disorders
- Depression
- Pain syndromes (fibromyalgia, chronic pain)

Increased activity in the DLS is often associated with depression, dysthymia, and negativity. Left-sided problems are often associated with anger and irritability, right-sided problems more often associated with inwardly directed sadness. In our experience we have seen that diffuse DLS overactivity tends to be more consistent with depression and focal increased DLS activity (more on one side than the other) tends to be associated with cyclic mood disorders. When focal increased uptake is found in conjunction with patchy increased uptake across the cortical surface, there is a higher likelihood of a cyclothymic or bipolar disorder.

5. Anxiety-driven: Using addictive substance and/or behavior as a way to soothe feelings of anxiety

- Active basal ganglia
- Addictions
- Anxiety disorders
- OCD
- Movement disorders
- Tourette's (tics)
- PTSD

Increased basal ganglia and insular activity is often associated with anxiety (left-side problems are often associated with irritability; right-side problems more often associated with inwardly directed anxiety).

6. Panic disorder temporal lobe: Using addictive substance and/or behavior as a way to soothe the self

- Low activity in temporal lobes
- Addictions
- Anxiety
- Aggression
- Dark thoughts
- Headaches
- Seizures
- Memory problems
- Abdominal complaints
- Illusions/paranoia
- Spaciness/confusion
- Learning problems

Abnormal TL (either increased or decreased) activity may be associated with mood instability, irritability, memory struggles, abnormal perceptions (auditory or visual illusions, periods of deja vu), periods of anxiety with little provocation, periods of spaciness or confusion, and unexplained headaches or abdominal pain. Left-side problems are more associated with irritability and dark thoughts, right-sided more with anxiety and social struggles. Anticonvulsant medications often help with TL problems. Decreased activity in the posterior aspects of the left temporal lobes, in our experience, is often, although not always, associated with language learning problems, especially reading and auditory processing problems. Memory loss is often associated with decreased activity in the medial temporal lobes.

MARIJUANA

The active ingredient in marijuana is THC, which stands for tetrahydrocannabinol. The human brain has THC receptor sites in several parts of the brain, with the majority of them being in the basal ganglia, temporal lobes, prefrontal cortex, and the limbic system. When a person uses marijuana, THC binds to the receptor sites in those parts of the brain and will either be an agonist or an antagonist in that part of the brain.

The problem with marijuana is that it floods the synapses with neurotransmitters and can cause damage to the neurotransmitter-producing sites and receptor sites. Considering where THC has the most amounts of receptor sites, the cognitive effects that people are likely to see are:

- Short-term memory loss

- Inattention
- Low motivation
- Anxiety
- Depression

Many times you will hear clients talk about how natural marijuana is and that there is no evidence that it causes any long-term problems. In fact, you will often hear them list every single therapeutic use of marijuana. There is clinical research that does support the medicinal use of marijuana. According to the Center for Medicinal Cannabis Research at the University of San Diego (2010), there are several effective medicinal uses of marijuana such as pain management, anti-nausea medication for chemo therapy patients, treatment for neuropathy associated with multiple sclerosis and other neurological disorders, and an effective sleep aid.

I am a man of science and cannot argue with that research, but the funny thing is how many of our failure-to-launch clients are battling cancer, multiple sclerosis, neuropathy, and so forth? None, zero, zip, zilch! Our clients will use research as a way to explain why it is okay for them to use these medications, but their argument is null and void because they do not have any of the conditions that it does effectively treat. Having them make an argument for marijuana use would be the same argument for them explaining why they take oxycontin on a regular basis. They can list every medical reason that it is used, but they do not have any of those conditions that it treats.

Since our clients do not have a medical rationale for using marijuana, they discuss how they use marijuana for the treatment of their anxiety, depression, and sleep problems. I have even heard clients give me a rationale that marijuana improves their attention/focus and they will get high before tests. They will attempt to cite research that supports it, but the problem is that the research does not support it. In fact, a recent study by a team of researchers led by Madeline Meier, PhD, appeared in the *Proceedings of the National Academy of Sciences* (2012) stating that chronic marijuana use in adolescence results in IQ drops in adulthood. In fact, the research shows that the earlier a child uses marijuana, the more it has a negative effect on IQ later in life.

Furthermore, SPECT and other forms of functional neuroimaging show that the earlier a person uses marijuana, the more it will have a damaging effect on brain tissue. Research by Wilson, Matthew, Turkington, Hawk, Coleman, and Provenzale (2000) showed that when people smoke marijuana before the age of seventeen, there was shrinkage in brain volume and reduction of cerebral blood flow in key areas of the brain. The earlier the use, the worse the shrinkage was.

What the research has showed us is that while the clients may be correct that when they smoke marijuana their anxiety and depressions levels go down, they do not realize that they are only temporarily fixing the problem and actually making it worse in the long run. I liken it to having a bruise on your arm. If you punch the bruise, the bruise gets worse. This is exactly what happens in the brain. The parts of the brain responsible for anxiety and depression do get down-regulated when people smoke marijuana. The problem is that it floods the synapses with neurotransmitters and will cause the producing sites to burn out and cause damage to the receptor sites. So they end up making their depression and anxiety worse over the long run.

This is the pattern that we see in failure-to-launch clients because they end up becoming dependent on marijuana to manage their symptoms, but they are smoking so much of it that they cannot function in life. It is a vicious cycle that is extremely difficult for them to get out of.

COCAINE AND OTHER AMPHETAMINES

Amphetamines are a class of drugs that have a stimulating effect on the brain and body. There are several different classifications of amphetamines that people abuse, but I will focus mainly on cocaine, ADHD medications, and methamphetamine. Amphetamines act on the brain by releasing high levels of dopamine as well as releasing neurotransmitters that prevent the re-uptake of dopamine. While most amphetamines have similar mechanisms in which they act on the brain, specific amphetamines have different receptor sites throughout the brain. The primary sites of action with amphetamines are the prefrontal cortex and the limbic system.

In controlled dosages, amphetamines are an effective way of improving attention, focus, motivation, and alertness. As we discussed in chapter 6, a lack of activity in the prefrontal cortex is the main culprit in inattention; so increasing dopamine levels in the prefrontal cortex is an effective way to manage symptoms of ADHD.

The problem that we run into with the failure-to-launch population is that our clients are not using their medications in accordance with what their doctors have laid out. Many are taking four to five times the amount that they are prescribed. Many even crush up the pills and snort them to get a more intense high. Prescription amphetamine abuse is a significant problem. The latest research suggests that as many as 9 percent of college students abuse stimulant medications either as a party drug or a study aid (Gomes, Song, Godwin, & Toriello, 2011).

When a person takes a medication that is either not prescribed for them or take dosages higher than what is prescribed, instead of fixing a problem they end up causing neurological damage. Instead of the drug helping make up for a deficit of dopamine, it will flood the synapses with dopamine and cause damage to the producing sites and the receptor sites. Ergo, if a person already had problems with inattention, they are now "making the bruise worse" and creating an even larger dopamine deficiency in parts of the brain. In clients who have no inattention problems who abuse these medications, then they literally can create inattention problems in the brain.

While prescription amphetamine abuse is rising, the good news is that illicit amphetamine use such as cocaine and methamphetamine is declining. According to the most recent figures by the National Survey on Drug Use and Health (2007), only 1.7 percent of people aged eighteen to twenty-five reported cocaine and methamphetamine abuse. This is a very promising statistic that drug education has worked, but it still is a problem with this population nonetheless.

While prescription stimulants are designed to only release certain quantities of dopamine, serotonin, and norepinephrine, cocaine, and methamphetamine release mass quantities of these neurotransmitters across every different type of neurotransmitter. I liken this to the metaphor of a smart bomb versus a conventional bomb. A smart bomb is designed to target a specific area with a specific yield. It can be guided and placed exactly where they want it to go with causing very little collateral damage. A conventional bomb is largely unguided and has a larger yield with very little control over how it causes damage. Prescription medications are like smart bombs with specific mechanisms to act on the brain, while drugs like cocaine and methamphetamine are conventional bombs with high explosive power and very little control.

When a person uses cocaine or methamphetamine, it floods the synapses in the prefrontal cortex and limbic system with dopamine, serotonin, and norepinephrine. Because it floods the synapses, it will cause the producing sites to burn out and will also cause damage to the receptor sites as well. Furthermore, the damage associated with methamphetamine is worse because of the nature of the chemical compounds used to manufacture methamphetamine. Chemicals such as benzene, ether, ammonia, red phosphorus, and toluene are used in the process. When a person uses methamphetamine, they are not only going to have the dangerous neurological damage caused by the amphetamine itself, but also the toxic damage caused from the other chemicals as well.

When we look at the damage caused by amphetamine abuse, we see significant damage to the outer cortical layers of the brain. Based on what we have seen in SPECT imaging and in clinical interviews, the following are typical side effects of chronic amphetamine abuse:

- Anxiety disorders
- Depressive disorders

- Paranoia
- Disturbances of thought
- Emotional lability
- Insomnia
- OCD behaviors (repetitive/compulsive behaviors: skin picking; taking items apart)
- Schizophrenia-like symptoms (e.g., hallucinations, disturbances of thought, delusional thinking)

What is scary about amphetamine abuse is that it short-circuits the dopamine reward system in the brain. The dopamine reward system is based in the frontal lobe of the brain and is based on the principle that when we do something good and receive a reward, dopamine releases in the brain and we feel good about ourselves. This feeling reinforces the behavior, and we continue to do it.

With cocaine and methamphetamine, it hijacks this system, and even when something bad happens (i.e., overdose, jail, etc.), the dopamine reward system is activated and will interpret even the most negative of events as a reward. This is why we believe the relapse rates are so high for methamphetamine, because all of the negatives that help keep most people from using again don't exist at all.

With failure to launch clients, amphetamine abuse is so difficult because every negative that happened in their life really is not apparent to them. When you try to point out all of the negatives of their use, it does not register with them, which usually continues the vicious cycle of enabling with the parents because they are waiting for their child to "get it" when they never will because of how the drugs work on their brain. Furthermore, amphetamine abuse complicates treatment because if they are having difficulty with attention, focus, and motivation, they have just exacerbated the problem and seriously handicapped themselves for future success.

OPIATES

Opiates are a class of drugs that act as nervous system depressant. The human body produces its own natural opioid compounds such as endorphins, enkephalins, and dynomorphin—collectively known as endogenous opioids. These neurochemicals help bind to parts of the brain that process pain and sensations. When a person experiences pain, the body naturally releases these neurotransmitters to help block the pain, ergo making the injury more bearable for the person.

While people have been using opiates for centuries, it was not until 1973 when the opioid receptor was identified by doctors. As a result of this discovery, new and more powerful synthetic opiate medications were developed to help with pain management. While this was indeed a great discovery, it opened a new area of substance abuse problems.

When we look at opiates, there are several different drugs that fit into this category. With prescription opiates, we have drugs such as morphine, hydrocodone, vicotin, codeine, oxycontin, opana, dilaudid, and fentanyl. The latter medications are newer and extremely powerful opiates that have been at the center of prescription drug abuse debates.

The main issue with prescription pain killers is that clients can get them every bit as easy as other illicit drugs. Many of our clients who struggle with prescription opiate addiction have a prescription for the medication or simply buy them from other people with prescriptions. One client disclosed that he was buying his hydrocodone pills from an elderly lady in his neighborhood who happened to be selling her medications to help make ends meet.

In addition to the many legal ways to get opiates, there are also the many illegal forms of the substance as well. Most of our clients report using powdered heroin which can be smoked, snorted, or used intravenously. There is also black tar heroin, which is mostly smoked. Lastly there is also a crystallized form of heroin called opium which is smoked as well. Many of our clients report that they initially started using prescription opiates, but once they developed a dependence on the substance, they would have to switch to illegal heroin because it's much cheaper to use and much easier to get than prescription opiates.

What is really important to understand with opiate abuse and our failure-to-launch clients is that since there are a large amount of opiate receptors in the emotional centers of the brain (limbic system), many of these clients are going to present with anxiety and depression symptoms. Many of our clients did not acknowledge any opiate abuse, rather instead reporting intense anxiety and debilitating depression. Once their use became apparent, many found it extremely difficult to quit because they could manage the physical withdrawal symptoms with drugs such as naltrexone or suboxone (drugs that act on the opiate receptors on the brain), but they could not handle the psychological withdrawal symptoms (anxiety and depression).

For the clients with intense withdrawal symptoms, inpatient detox and residential treatment might be their only option to stay clean or to stay safe while they manage their psychological symptoms. For some clients who have been clean for several months, they still find it difficult to manage their psychological symptoms. Brain imaging has helped us understand that opiates ravage the receptor sites in the brain creating a permanent short-fall of important mood stabilizing neurotransmitters such as dopamine, serotonin, and norepinepherine. When the brain is in short supply of these chemicals, the brain will often be underactive/overactive in certain parts and will cause significant problems in psychological functioning (i.e., depression, anxiety, inattention, etc.).

This is really important to understand because for clients who have abused opiates for a long period of time, their brain might have irreversible brain damage, and they might struggle with intense anxiety/depression for the rest of their lives. Living independently might be a struggle for them and might be the culprit in the client's failure-to-launch problem.

III

Moving the Immovable Object

Chapter Nine

Why Change? What's My Motivation to Change?

When I begin to see a family, I often get asked the question, "How do you work with an adult client and his or her family?" Many parents express concern over protecting their children's confidentiality and fear that if I work with them, their child will not trust me and will shut down. I often tell parents that this is a valid concern, and I work very hard to create a safe and confidential working alliance with my clients and will not divulge any information that will jeopardize that relationship.

I cannot stress how important the working relationship is with clients in this population. Most of these clients have been in therapy several times and have a negative view of therapists and the therapy process. Often, I will have parents say that they normally can never get their children in for counseling and are not sure what to tell them to motivate them to come in. What I usually tell parents is to say to their child that they found a counselor/life coach that wants to help give them life and career coaching—somebody who is there to help them make better decisions and to help them figure out what they want to do with their life. I even have parents tell their children that I will help coach the parents on how to help the situation better rather than hurt it.

This usually gets the client in to my office and buys me at least a session or two to build rapport and learn to trust me and my process. In a perfect world, I will use the techniques in the next few chapters to help create internal motivation for change. Getting the clients to motivate themselves without getting too much into the family system is always my preferred option. But what I tell parents is that if I cannot get any progress working with the client individually, then we must provide external pressure on the client to get them to change.

This is a tricky maneuver because with an adult client, HIPPA prevents us from divulging any confidential information without the client's permission. Furthermore, it will also shatter the patient-client relationship if the client feels as though you are working behind his back with the family. It is not easy to dance around these issues, but it is a necessity to do this because ultimately we need to get these children launched in to the future. If they are unwilling to do this themselves, then we have to make sure the family system adjusts to ensure that it happens. Remember what I said in the beginning of this book, sometimes a parent has to let a child fail to succeed.

With that in mind, the following chapter will focus on the techniques that I have used in practice to successfully launch my clients in to the future. We will begin by looking at the techniques that you will utilize to create internal motivation for change, how we can use tools to help map out a successful future for each client, and how to incorporate life coaching and counseling techniques to guide our clients on their journey. Secondly, I will lay out a clear, step-by-step procedure to work with the family and how to help re-structure family systems to help not only launch their children into the future, but also how to prevent them from falling back into the same negative cycle again.

One of my favorite conversations that I have with a client is when we start to discuss motivation. Usually in the first or second session, I will hear a client talk about his or her difficulty getting the energy or motivation to work or go to school. Some of my clients even discuss the difficulty in finding the motivation to get out of bed and shower. When I ask my clients how they define motivation, I usually get some type of answer that involves describing a trait that they want but just don't have . . . almost describing it like it's a missing bodily organ or something. I always laugh on the inside when I hear their descriptions. For some reason I find it amusing to hear a client describe motivation as some esoteric concept that everybody has but them. Sitting here and thinking about it, I guess I find it funny because it's a complete load of crap.

While my colleagues may laugh at me, I usually tell clients that I understand their frustration and follow up with that I think their definition of motivation is bull$hi%. You may think I may be joking but usually that's what I tell my clients . . . albeit with it a smile on my face so that they do not take offense.

I say this to them because their idea of motivation is bull$hi%, and I want them to know it. Let me explain so that you don't get the wrong idea. When we are confronted with a decision to do something, we make a decision either to do it or to not do it. When I was eighteen years old, I was confronted with a decision to either get drunk with my roommates or sit down and do my homework. I did not want to do my homework, and drinking with my friends sounded much more fun, so I decided to do that with my friends instead. It had nothing to do with my inability to force myself to sit down and do my homework; it came down to a choice. It is the same exact thing with our clients.

When we have a client telling us how they really planned to go to class this morning but when they got up, they just did not have the motivation to get out of bed and make it to class. They will really try to sell you on their frustration too. They will almost make it sound like they were tied down in their bed and they didn't have the key to get out.

As a clinician, we have two choices at this point. We can empathize with them and reinforce their powerlessness from not having the motivation organ, or we can call bull$hi% and call it out for what it really is. I choose to call them out for what it really is . . . which is a choice. It was not a lack of motivation that kept them in bed, it was a choice. They made the choice in their head that it was easier and more comfortable to lay in bed rather than get up and go to class. Motivation is a bull$hi% concept with our clients, they simply make conscious choices to not do the things they do not want to do.

We have to call our clients out because they buy into their bull$hi%. It is a form of learned helplessness that reduces that cognitive dissonance that results when they do the opposite of what they know they should do. We all know it's wrong to be lazy, skip class, get drunk the night before a test, and so forth. If we consciously make this decision, it creates cognitive dissonance, anxiety, negative emotions, and so forth. So clients reduce this dissonance by claiming it's something beyond their control. By calling our clients out, we get them to see their decision making, thought processes, schemas, and actions for what they really are . . . a conscious decision. By getting our clients to realize this, we have helped them take the first step in the direction of launching into their future.

The only problem is that this realization, albeit huge, is only the first step in a long process. All we have done is gotten the client to admit that they are lazy and taking the path of least resistance. When confronted with the same decisions again at this point, the majority of them will just make a conscious decision to not go to class. So where do we begin . . . how do we begin to motivate these clients?

Since I have been working with these clients for almost ten years now, I have tried everything under the sun to bring about internal change in these clients. Some clients will respond to reasoning with them and giving them a pep-talk, but most clients will still be stuck in their stubborn ways. I have a colleague in my practice that said it best. When you have a client at this stage of therapy/coaching, they are either willful or willing when it comes to change. Most clients are willful when it comes to change; meaning that they have a true desire to change. However, many are not willing, meaning that while they have the desire to change, they do not have the willingness to make the decisions or take the actions necessary to change.

Whether it is an entitled child who takes the path of least resistance or the anxious/depressed client who is fearful of failure, the only technique that has consistently worked to bring about true internal change is motivational interviewing.

So what exactly is motivation interviewing or MI? MI was first mentioned in 1983 by William R. Miller, PhD, who was describing a hybrid person-centered and semi-directive technique to work with problem drinkers. The technique focused on the problem drinkers' resistance to change their behaviors and attempted to work through that resistance to help increase positive outcomes with this population. The technique was later elaborated on by William Miller, PhD, and Stephen Rollick, PhD (1991). According to motivationinterview.org (2009), the most recent definition of MI is "a collaborative, person-centered form of guiding to elicit and strengthen motivation for change." Moreover, MI "is a collaborative, goal-oriented method of communication with particular attention to the language of change. It is designed to strengthen an individual's motivation for and movement toward a specific goal by eliciting and exploring the person's own arguments for change."

While MI was initially developed to work with problem drinkers, its efficacy with such a difficult population led many to experiment with other difficult populations such as people with substance and process addictions. In the past ten years, MI use has grown drastically with many different professions utilizing its approach; most notably has been the medical and health insurance community.

Medical schools have increasingly been teaching their medical students MI techniques as a means to gather important clinical data about their clients, build better doctor-patient rapport, and promote more positive/healthy behaviors with their clients. For example, doctors are using these techniques to help motivate their patients to make difficult changes in their lives such as losing weight, quitting smoking, and exercising. Health insurance companies have also jumped on the bandwagon and have developed case management programs that utilize MI techniques to work with clients to make similar positive/healthy changes in their lives, thus bringing down health care costs.

Rollick and Miller explain that MI is a perspective that emphasizes the following:

1. The acceptance of applied labels such as addict or alcoholic is not a pre-requisite for change.
2. Treatment is a personal choice.
3. The individual is responsible for change.
4. Resistance should be viewed as a relationship of influence by the therapist's attitude or behavior toward the individual.

5. Encourages collaborative treatment planning.
6. Views ambivalence versus denial as a central treatment issue.

The beautiful thing about motivational interviewing is that positive outcome does not hinge on whether or not your client wants to admit that they have a problem or that they have to accept the labels that are being applied to them. Many clients will talk you in circles when you try to label them as an addict or depressed. You will spend an entire session just talking about the label, and nothing will actually get done. The client's defenses will be triggered, and their willingness to listen to insight and reason is out the door. In MI, the client does not have to admit it, therefore as clinicians we do not have to spend much time on clinical labels or diagnosis with these patients.

Another great thing about MI is that the individual is responsible for change, not the therapist or the client's parents. So many times a client will talk about all of the reasons for why they cannot succeed and will placate much of the blame for their problems. In this approach we put the onus of change squarely on the shoulders of the client. Moreover, we also make treatment a personal choice; either they want to make the changes in their lives or they do not. Lastly, because we are working with a difficult population that is often ambivalent about change or in denial about the need to change, this dynamic plays a central role in MI and will often be the focus of conversations and sessions.

When we look at it in practice, it is more a set of "technical interventions" rather than a psychological orientation on its own. The "spirit" of MI is rooted in three elements: collaboration, evocation, and autonomy. In MI terms, collaboration is a process in which we explore the worldview and experiences of the client. This is a very important part of MI because many times our clients have been invalidated by their parents and even past professionals. They are almost waiting on us to correct them or tell them that their beliefs are irrational. In MI, it is our job to explore and understand what the world looks like through their eyes, nothing more, and nothing less.

Evocation in MI terms is for the therapist to evoke or pull-out the client's thoughts and ideas rather than impose those ideas on the clients. When we explore the client's worldview, certain themes will begin to emerge about their own goals and ideas for change. Our job is not to come up with their goals for them; we simply act as a facilitator to help pull those goals out themselves. Since the client is responsible for their own change, their goals must be their own, not the therapist's or their parents.

Lastly, autonomy in MI terms is the idea that reinforces that the power to change is solely within the client. It is important to help the client understand that they have to make the decision to change and there is no right or wrong way to change. There are several ways to achieve their goals, and they can choose what goals and what order they will achieve them.

While the "spirit" of MI is used to help bring to life the process of MI, it is the four principles of MI that guide the actual process. The four principles of MI are expressing empathy, supporting self-efficacy, rolling with resistance, and developing discrepancy.

The very first step in the process of MI is expressing empathy with the client. In MI terms, this is the process of exploring the worldview of the client and attempting to understand how the client experiences themselves and the world around them. It is very important to empathize with the client and try to understand their troubles rather than try to point out to them what they are doing wrong. It is at this stage of MI where we begin to develop rapport with the client and begin to gather clinical information as to why they are struggling to make changes in their lives and what their own personal goals are.

Many times at this stage of treatment, you will begin to see patterns behavior that contradict what their goals are. While you may feel a strong urge to point out these contradictions, this is not the time to point them out. You simply take down all the relevant information and make notes to come back to these at a later time. Remember, a client is used to people telling them everything that they are doing wrong and how they have failed in life. Part of the beginning process is to empathize with them and build a collaborative relationship that makes them feel as though you are working with them and not judging them. Any attempt to bring about change at this stage will only trigger their defenses and will drive a wedge in between yourself and your client, as well as preventing them from making any significant changes in their life.

Furthermore, when we empathize with the client at this stage, it develops a secure base from which a client will honestly explore their thoughts and feelings, allowing them to be vulnerable with the therapist. I cannot stress how important this is to the process because our clients often experience high levels of shame with their behaviors and have rarely been honest with themselves let alone anybody else. If we create an environment where they feel as though they will not be judged, they will slowly take changes in your sessions and will open up to you. Additionally, this will help you later in your sessions when we begin to give difficult feedback about their behaviors; especially if they are not making progress. Instead of taking the feedback as an attack, they look at you as somebody who really is trying to help them and will take the feedback as constructive and honest.

The process of expressive empathy often is an ongoing process that will be utilized throughout the MI process. However, the initial information gathering should last a few sessions with sufficient rapport being built up during that time to start moving on in the MI process. It is important to note that clients with more pathological issues such as depression, anxiety, Asperger's, and so forth will be more difficult to work with, and more time will probably need to be spent in this phase of treatment.

After sufficient information is gathered and a secure base has been established, we can begin to proceed into the next phase of MI which is supporting self-efficacy. Remember, one of the most important principles in MI is that the client is responsible for change. It is in this stage of treatment that we work on getting our clients to believe that they do have the power to make changes in their lives and achieve their goals.

By the times that we see these clients, they often are defeated and believe that they do not have the ability to be successful in their lives. The clients are stuck in a negative feedback cycle in their family systems and have not heard any positive feedback in months, sometimes years. While some clients will have fully embraced learned helplessness, many truly believe that they are not capable of being successful.

Since our clients only really know failure up to this point, it is important to help direct the clients to the successes that they have had in life. To borrow a term from Albert Ellis, many clients often wear the "shit covered goggles," meaning that they only see all of their failures and negative attributes. Our job at this point in treatment is to help them realize that they have had successes and they do have several strengths. We point these out to the client to help them realize that they do have the ability to succeed, and we use those strengths to help them overcome their weaknesses. Once a client begins to buy in to their strengths, they start to believe that they may have the ability to change.

I recall a very touching moment with one of my clients where we were talking about school, and the client expressed every negative thought that he had about his scholastic abilities and even recalled several teachers telling him that he shouldn't go to college because he would not be able to do it. I visibly saw him sinking lower in to his chair when he was going through all of his negative thoughts, and it really affected me.

Here in front of me was a 6'0" 280 lbs. man slowly shrinking in front of me due to the weight of all the negative beliefs he had about himself. But what was interesting about this guy who allegedly "could never succeed in school" was that he was a successful writer and recruiter for a college football website. He never had any formal training, and he was outperforming all of his older, more educated, and more seasoned counterparts. When I began to point out these facts to the client and reframed it in terms of different types of intelligence, I brought it back to the point that these facts actually predict intelligence which in-turn predicts success in school, work, or whatever else he wants to do. I told him that he could be successful in whatever he wanted to do and that if he chooses school, we will figure out a method to help him be successful. I remember seeing his eyes well up with tears, and he said to me that nobody ever told him that he could be successful in school. He was literally blown away that he could be successful in school, and for the first time in his life, he believed that he was a capable person who could do whatever he wanted.

This is the power of MI and how it really affects our clients on a deep level. When conducted properly, it can really help clients make paradigm shifts in their schemas/internal-working models. While paradigm shifts like this are very powerful experiences for the client and the therapist, there still are several roadblocks that prevent clients from taking a paradigm shift into action. This is why the next phase of MI focuses on rolling with resistance.

In MI terms, resistance is when the client experiences a disagreement between their view or solution to the problem and the therapist's view or solution to the problem. In MI, the client has the freedom to make their own choices about moving forward, and typically a client will express some type of resistance when they feel as though that freedom or autonomy is being infringed upon. In most cases, the resistance mostly has to do with a client's ambivalence to make changes in their lives.

Think about it like this, I had a client who was setting personal goals to get good grades in school and wanted to not skip any of his classes. When push came to shove, he began to realize how difficult it was for him to make it to class every day. He began to waffle about going to college and even suggested that he drop out and that college was not for him. The client even started to blame his parents for pressuring him to go to school. He began to experience resistance that was based on his ambivalence to actually make the changes necessary to be successful in school (i.e., getting up every day, doing homework, studying, etc.).

When a client begins to express resistance to change, we simply roll with the resistance. Instead of challenging the client and trying to get them to change their mind, simply empathize with their struggle and try to help them through their ambivalence. If we start to challenge their ambivalence, then a struggle can ensue between the therapist and the client. This usually results in a session of a client "yes butting" you to death or trying to play devil's advocate to anything that you will say. Especially during the early sessions, you must be careful to avoid this dynamic and just roll with whatever they give you. Allowing the client to come up with their own solutions to their problems leaves them very little to resist in therapy. This dynamic can clearly be seen between parents and their children.

Parents will often let their children come up with their own solutions, but as soon as the plan hits a roadblock, they begin to question their child's plan, and it ensues into a struggle between mom and dad's solutions versus the child's. More often than not, the client will dig their heels in and will play the role of an obstinate child and do the opposite of what mom and dad want. The client will often take actions that go directly against what their stated goals are just to prove a point. I often call this "cutting off your face to spite your nose."

The last and in my mind the most effective part of MI is developing discrepancy. In MI terms, developing discrepancy is the process of pointing out the dissonance that exists between a client's stated goals and what their current behaviors are. So many times, clients will say that they want to get straight A's in school, but when you look at their behavior, they are smoking pot every day and playing video games until 2:00 a.m. The stated goals of the clients are mutually exclusive with their current behavior. In MI, it is not our job to tell them what they are doing is wrong. What our job is to point out to them that they cannot accomplish their stated goals with the current behavior that they are doing. By pointing out the discrepancy between these two things, it motivates that client to makes the changes necessary in their lives to succeed or to bring their behavior more in line with what their values are.

For example, I was working with a client who was experiencing sex addiction problems; most notably using pornography and visiting prostitutes. Instead of telling him that he was doing illegal things and that he was sinning, which is what his previous counselor told him, I simply presented him with the following:

> *Bob, so on one hand you say that you want to be more involved in the church, be a better boyfriend, and try to be more successful in your career. Those are great goals, goals that I think many people that would have for themselves. But on the other hand, you are visiting prostitutes which makes you feel guilt and pulls you farther away from your girlfriend as well as potentially getting into legal issues that will directly affect your job, and you are using pornography which also makes you feel guilty and makes you not want to go to church because you feel like an imposter. Now, it's not my job to say what you should or shouldn't do but it seems like your current actions are in direct conflict with what your goals are. I don't think you can accomplish your goals and continue your current behavior. What do you think about that?*

After presenting that to the client, he replied to me that it was impossible for him to continue doing the same things and accomplish the goals that he wants. He realized at the moment that he needed to change what he was doing and for the first time in his life, he was motivated to make changes in his life. Now there were many obstacles that we encountered along the way, but he was motivated enough to plow through the obstacles that came his way.

When utilizing the techniques of MI, you will find that there is not a singular way of going through the process with each client. You will realize that it is a living and breathing technique that you will adapt for use with your clients. Furthermore, once you move through one phase of MI, you will have to keep going back to each technique as obstacles and ambivalence creep up.

What also is great about MI is that since it is more of a technique rather than a psychotherapeutic theory, ergo you can integrate MI with your favorite therapeutic background (CBT, psychodynamic, DBT, etc.). For the purpose of saving time, I will not cover psychotherapeutic theories in this book but will rather focus later chapters on career/life coaching and family systems work.

Chapter Ten

"What Do You Want to Do Now That You Are Grown Up?"

I think one of the most important decisions that a young adult makes is deciding what they want to do for their career. When I was a kid, most of my classmates had no idea what they wanted to do until their senior year. Many just planned to go to Ohio State University and figure out what their major was going to be after their freshman year. But times have changed since then.

Children as young as middle school are taking practice SAT/ACT tests and are busy building up their resumes in their freshman year. Today's students are under so much pressure to perform that even a high 3.something GPA is not even good enough to get into certain state schools. In Texas, high school students have to finish in the top 10 percent of their class to get in to the University of Texas; with that number changing to the top 8 percent in the following years.

What is amazing to me is that despite this pressure, many students take that pressure head on. When I speak to these students who are achieving at a very high level, I found a pattern developing in their responses. The pattern that I noticed was that every single one of these students knew exactly what they wanted to do. I am not even talking about being a doctor, I am talking about what kind of doctor they wanted to be. In a recent presentation that I did at a local school, I spoke to one student with a 4.3 GPA who said that he wanted to get his PhD in biochemical engineering so that he could be a scientist that helps create new kinds of medicines. Another student who had a 4.25 GPA said that she wanted to be a plastic surgeon so that she could help repair facial deformities in children and third-world citizens.

These kids spend countless hours outside of school doing homework, writing papers, studying, volunteering, school activities, and so forth; and they never look back or question what it is that they are doing. They all realize how difficult it is to maintain a high level of academic achievement and even admit how stressed out they are; but they keep going. When I ask them what keeps them going, they commonly reply that the pain is worth their ultimate career goal. They would rather give 110 percent now so they can reap the rewards of a great career later.

I often refer to this mind-set as the "Shawshank Redemption Mind-set." In the movie *Shawshank Redemption*, Andy Dufresne is a banker who was wrongly accused of murdering his wife and was sentenced to prison for life. Andy never was able to come to grips with the fact that he would be stuck in jail for a crime he never committed, so he slowly plotted his escape over fifteen years. At the end of the movie, the only thing that stood between him and freedom was a three hundred-yard sewage pipe filled with human excrement. Andy crawled through that pipe, and he made his way to freedom.

I always use this example when I speak to my failure-to-launch clients because I ask them, "Why did Andy crawl through that river? What made it worth it to him?" Most of clients respond that it was worth crawling through a river of crap because his freedom made it worth it. I then ask them, "Would you have done the same thing?" Once again, my clients answer that they would be willing to crawl through the pipe because the freedom was worth it.

The reason I do this with my clients is to make a point, that if there is something that you want really bad, you would be willing to go through anything for it, even crawl through a pipe filled with crap. This is important to understand because with our failure-to-launch clients, many of them do not want to put any effort in to their work, whether it is doing homework, going to class, studying for tests, and so forth. They just do not have the desire to go through the pain of doing those things. There are other things that they want to do with their life that are more fun and satisfying.

What I found with many of these clients is that when I ask them what they want to do with their lives, many of them have no idea. Even when I ask them whether they have ever had an idea what they wanted to do for a career, many of them either say no or they thought that they did but after a short amount of time, lost interest. To many of our clients, crawling through a pipe filled with crap is the perfect metaphor for going through school and being successful. If we are borrowing this metaphor, then asking these clients to crawl through this pipe with little or nothing on the other end is pointless . . . they have nothing at the other end to help get them through it.

This is something that I can totally relate to. When I dropped out of flying, I had absolutely no idea what I wanted to do with my life. I did not have any career goal that made it worth being a good student and giving up having fun. It is not coincidental that as soon as I figured out what I wanted to do with my life, I started becoming more motivated to go to school and do what was needed to be a good student.

This is why I believe that having career goals is an essential part to being successful in life. It not only helps provide the motivation to get through the difficult times, but it also provides a direction for a client to go in. Think about it like this . . . if I were to turn to you and say let's go on a trip, your natural response would be to ask where. If I don't give you a destination, how would you know what road to take, what direction to go in, how to pack, and so forth?

The same thing goes for our clients as well. If they do not know where they are going, how do they know what college to go to, how to prepare, what part of the country to be in, what jobs to get, and so forth? A failure-to-launch client needs to understand what their career is going to be so that they know what steps they need to take and in what order to take them.

So how do we help our clients figure out the life-defining question of "What do you want to do now that you are grown up?" If only it were as simple as asking a question and getting an answer from them. The problem for many of these clients is that they have either no idea what they want to do or they know what they want to do and have zero confidence in accomplishing it. With the latter, I have found that many of my clients will express aloud that they have no idea what they want to do. This complicates the picture because many clinicians and parents will proceed with basic career exploration rather than attempt to understand where their lack of confidence arises.

The process in which I have the most confidence in helping a client explore and uncover their true career goals is through vocational assessment. So what exactly makes up a vocational assessment? Every clinician probably has their own personal preference in what they include in a vocational assessment, so I will spend this chapter speaking to my personal preference.

Before you give any assessments, the very first step in any good vocational assessment is a good clinical interview. Many clinicians have asked me why I put so much emphasis on a clinical interview. The reason that I do in these cases is that the depth and quality of information that you can gather during a clinical interview is second to none. Furthermore, the data that you collect with your vocational instruments will be worthless without having the context of the information you gather during clinical assessment.

In my clinical interviews, I use a semi-structured approach; meaning that I do not have any specific order in which I ask my questions, but I make sure that I ask specific questions every single time. Here is a list of the questions that I make sure I ask during my clinical interviews:

1. What are some of your general interests?
2. What are you passionate about in life?
3. Have you ever had any idea of what you wanted to do in your life, even when you were a young child?
4. What are your thoughts about college?

5. When do you want to arrive in your career (i.e., at what age do you want to be in your first job)?
6. What is the longest amount of time you are willing to go to school if at all?
7. When you think about the future, what types of things do you absolutely need in your life (i.e., size of house, kinds of cars, vacations, toys, and so forth . . .)?
8. How much money do you want to make?
9. What types of environments do you like to work in most/work in least?
10. Do you like working with people?
11. What were your favorite subjects in school?
12. What were your worst subjects in school?
13. What were your grades like in school?
14. What do your parents/family members do for a living? What do you know/think about their careers?

By no means is this an exhaustive list of questions to ask your clients, but I think this is a great baseline to get the information that you need to help understand your client and how to define the data that you get from the assessments.

There are many reasons why I ask the questions that I do in my clinical interviews. The two questions that yield the most useful data are "How long do you want to go to school" and "When do you want to arrive in your career." I like these questions because they will really help you single out specific career choices more than any other question. For example, if a client responds with, "I only want to go to school for a maximum of four years," we know that any type of career that requires graduate studies is off the table. What if a client says that they are only willing to go to school for two years? Then we know that we are looking more at professional schools rather than a traditional college. I have had clients in my office who said that they wanted to be a doctor, but when I say how much schooling and training is involved with being a doctor, then they immediately say that they had no idea and would rather choose some other career. The amount of school and training that a person is willing to go through will make or break a particular career.

Two other questions that will generate a lot of data are "How much money do you want to make?" and "What types of things do you need in your life?" I love these questions because if a client says that they want to make $300,000 a year, then we automatically know that we have to start looking at careers that will afford them that type of living. Whereas if the client says that money is not important and as long as they make $65,000 per year they will be happy, we know that we can choose a career and money does not really factor in.

Many times my clients have been living off of their parents and have no concept of money and how much they want to make. That is why I ask what kinds of things they want when they get older, because that will give me an idea of how much money they need to make to support those things. For instance, if a person says they want a big house, sports car, boat, and go on great vacations, I automatically know that they will need a high-paying job to support it and will help explore those types of jobs with the client.

The last question that I will comment on is what their grades were in school. As I explained in the beginning of this chapter, college is more competitive than it ever has been before. If I have a student who has breezed through the first year or two of college with B/C's, I know that we have a limited amount of time to get their grades to improve. The truth of the matter is that if you have a student with grades in this range, certain career fields are going to be very difficult for them to get in to. If they choose a field that requires graduate school, they very well may not have grades good enough to get into a program. When I was applying to doctoral programs, the acceptance rate was one-third, meaning that only one-third of applicants to doctoral programs were getting accepted. The rates for law school and medical school are even smaller. While I am not one to shoot down a client's dreams, we do have an obligation to be honest with them and let them know if they are choosing a career path that they virtually have no chance of getting in to.

A typical clinical interview should take you about 1 to 1.5 hours. What I typically do is conduct this interview during the first session and will continue it during the second session if I find that I did not get all the information that I wanted.

With the clinical interview out of the way, the next phase of assessment is the actual instruments. I only use two instruments in my assessments: the Myers-Briggs Type Indicator (MBTI) and the Strong Interest Inventory (SII).

The MBTI is a psychological questionnaire that is designed to measure a person's preferences in how they experience the world around them and how they make decisions. The preferences in the MBTI are based on Carl Jung's personality typologies. The test was developed by Dr. Katharine Briggs and Dr. Isabel Myers during World War II. The test was used as a means to help find the proper placement for women in industrial jobs to help aid in the war effort. The questionnaire first appeared as the "Myers-Briggs" in 1962 and has been touted as one of the most widely used personality assessments.

The MBTI is based on four main dichotomies: introversion/extroversion, sensing/intuition, thinking/feeling, and judging/perceiving. What I really love about the MBTI is that it is not so much a measure of personality characteristics but more a measure of personality style. This is very important for us to understand in vocational assessment because not only are we interested in finding a career that matches a person's interests, but also a career that matches their personality style. For example, if we have a client who is outgoing, gregarious, sociable, hates routine, and likes an open approach to life, then having them choose a quiet data entry desk job would be a disaster for them. They would be miserable and looking for a new career within a short amount of time.

This is why I always give the feedback for the MBTI first because in order to help guide our clients in picking the career that is right for them, we have to get a better idea of who they are and in what environments they would be most effective and satisfied in.

When giving the MBTI feedback, I always begin by reading the description of each dichotomy and I ask them which one they fall under. It is really important to clearly explain what each dichotomy is and how it relates to them. I usually pull information from their clinical interview to help illustrate to them why they are successful in certain areas of life and why they struggle in others. Moreover, be sure to explain their MBTI styles in terms of career, explaining the information in ways to show what types of environments they would be most successful in and what types of jobs they would be most happy in.

After giving the MBTI feedback, discuss the results with the client and make sure they understand the results that you just gave them and, see if they have any questions. Most of my clients feel as though the MBTI was very accurate and start to have insights into some of the reasons why they are having career indecision. It is at this point that we put the MBTI behind and move on to the SII feedback.

The SII was first developed in 1927 by Dr. EK Strong to help World War I veterans find placement after the war. The SII went through many developmental changes throughout the years with the most updates coming at the hands of Dr. David Campbell. The modern version of the SII is rooted in Dr. John Holland's vocational theory or vocational codes. Holland's codes are based on different areas of occupational interest that match up to people's personality types. The Holland codes are as follows: realistic (doers), investigative (thinkers), artistic (creators), social (helpers), enterprising (persuaders), and conventional (organizers).

How I explain the SII to my clients is that it is an assessment that is based on the theory that we will be happiest working in a career that matches most closely with our personal interests and personality traits. What this assessment does is ask a series of questions that will determine where your interests lie and will then explore the possible careers within that interest area.

Depending on the company that you go through for your assessment, there are several different versions of the test that you can use. Depending on your client, you can choose the SII for high school populations, college populations, professional populations, or just a standard SII administration. Furthermore, you can choose several different options with your results such as a standard profile; standard profile with interpretive report; or standard profile, interpretive report, with the skills confidence inventory. I highly recommend you get all three because the data is highly useful in all three results and the interpretive report gives the client much more information to take home with them.

So what do the results look like in the SII? If you get all three reports, you will get the following information:

1. Scores on the level of interest on each of the 6 Holland Codes or general occupational themes.
2. Scores on 30 basic interest scales (e.g., art, science, and public speaking).
3. Scores on 244 occupational scales which indicate the similarity between the respondent's interests and those of people working in each of the 122 occupations.
4. Scores on 5 personal style scales (learning, working, leadership, risk-taking, and team orientation).
5. Scores on 3 administrative scales used to identify test errors or unusual profiles.
6. Scores on the skills confidence scale.

Just as I said with the MBTI feedback, any idiot can just go through these results and say, "Well it says here you are an artistic person and your number one occupation on the occupational scale is art teacher . . . so let's just go with that." There is much more to the SII results than that, so I will give you an idea of how I use the SII data in my feedback sessions.

The first thing I start off with is that I explain the Holland Occupational Scales and read each one to them. I then ask them what they think their results were. I think it is good to do this because if it's similar, then it gives you a talking point of how in tune with their interests they are. If their guess is dissimilar, then it gives you a talking point of why there is incongruence with their reported occupational theme.

What I do next is go through what their occupational codes are and explore what their initial reactions are and what they know about the possible jobs within that interest area. When there is a high level of interest in the occupational codes, it makes our jobs much easier. But you will get some clients who have very moderate interest in all of the areas, and further exploration will be needed. Much of your work with these clients will be pulling information out of the basic interest scales and the occupational scales.

After exploring the general occupational themes, we then move on to the basic interest scales. I really like these scales because it takes the client from looking at general levels of interests and starts to open up the career possibilities within each interest area. I usually start exploring the career area that they have the most interest in and begin to explore each basic interest area with the client. I will ask questions about what they know about the interest area, and we will use the computer to search all the careers that fall into it.

After going through each interest area, you should have a nice sized list of possible career areas to explore further with your client. With this list, I will go over each career field and explore very possible iteration of jobs. For example, if a client were to have a very high level of interest in performing arts under the artistic interest area, we would explore all the careers that are considered performing arts. The best way to do this is to go to www.onetonline.org which is a free career exploration tool that you can use to explore career fields with your clients. Simply go to the website, type in performing arts, and every major job within that area will come up. If you click on a particular job, it will list the education required, average salary, job requirements, and so forth.

With each job, we will explore the ins and outs of the job and will see what the clients reactions are. With each career field we have flagged on our notes, we will repeat this process until we have a short list of jobs and career fields that are potential matches for the client.

This is usually a very exciting process because you get to see the client get enthusiastic about jobs they never knew existed. You take a client who had no idea what they wanted to do with their life and all of a sudden they see multiple options right in front of them.

There are many options that you can take at this point with the remaining SII data. The next section of the SII takes all of the interests that your client had and matched them up with specific careers that people reported being happy in. This is a nifty little section that can help you out if your client had no real clear areas of interest in the previous section. While the information is useful, I tend to gloss over this section because the specific jobs that it provides are actually what we find on onetonline and it really is redundant information if you take that step. Furthermore, a lot of the jobs can be very random, and I find that it reduces the usefulness for the client.

The same goes for the five personal styles scales section on the SII. Since we already went over personal style with the MBTI results, I find that the information is largely redundant and that I would rather spend our limited session time on other items.

The last major item that I look at is the Skills Confidence Scale. I really like this scale because it is the last bit of information that can give you alternative areas to explore with your client. What this scale looks at is your overall confidence within a particular interest area and matches it up against your confidence in that area. This is very useful because sometimes a client will have turned down opportunities in a particular career field because of a lack of perceived confidence in the area. This is why they have career indecision because the only thing they want to do, they perceive that they won't succeed. This scale gives us information to determine if that is going on in certain interest areas and allows us the ability to coach our clients and see if we can build up their confidence in that area.

After all is said and done with our clinical interview, vocational assessments, and career exploration, we have a short list of possible career fields in which we can choose from. The best thing to do at this time is to send your client home with all of the information and have them speak to their families or spouses about the options that they have in front of them. The last thing that I do with my client during this phase is to ask them how they feel. I do this because it's important to gauge how they feel after digesting all of this information. Many times I get the answer "I feel good, I feel like I have something here that I can choose from." I love when I hear that because I know that the process is working for them and they begin to see options.

Now that we have specific options for our clients, the tough work begins of coaching them through a decision and not only setting up a plan for how to accomplish their new career goal, but also coaching them through the process step by step if necessary. The next chapter will focus on coaching and counseling our clients through this process.

Chapter Eleven

Career and Life Coaching

With many of our clients, simply showing them the way is not enough to get them to where they need to go. A lot of these clients have had everything done for them their whole life and were just never taught how to accomplish things on their own. For others, they simply have no idea of how to get from point A to point B. It is for this reason that we cannot assume they know how to get there and instead shift our thinking and assume that they do not know how to get there and therefore need help, guidance, coaching, and even cheerleading.

When I was in graduate school, I was fortunate enough to have an internal practicum at the UNT Counseling and Testing Center. It was here where I was taught the art of vocational assessment and the usefulness of coaching our clients rather than counseling them. I recall a group supervision with the director of the center, and he told us that if we trust our clients to go home and do the homework we assign them, then we will never make any progress with our clients. He bluntly told us that we have on average of four sessions to get some type of change with our clients; therefore we must maximize all the available time that we have with them.

With his very honest assertions, I began to realize the importance of coaching our clients rather than counseling them, especially when we were dealing with a non-clinical population. So instead of doing traditional talk therapy and cognitive-behavioral counseling, I took a more proactive approach with my clients, set goals, and worked on the various goals actually in my office. Many times we would get on the computer together and look at career resources, community resources, and even helped clients look for jobs.

What I found was that if you gave them homework to look over the career resources and bring in what they found, maybe 40 percent of the time they would do the homework. Of that 40 percent, maybe 50 percent actually put in a real effort on the homework.

When I decided to go in to private practice, I was going to be different and put emphasis on coaching as much as counseling. So how exactly do I delineate between coaching and counseling? I tend to view counseling as the process where we conceptualize our clients in a psychological construct and apply the principles of whichever therapeutic background we adhere to. I tend to view coaching as a collaborative process between the clinician and the client. I believe that coaching differs from counseling in the aspect that the clinician who is doing coaching will be much more involved with helping the client change than in counseling. In coaching, the clinician will make phone calls with the client in the office, get on the computer and actually look up things with the client, and even go out into the community with the client to ensure that progress is being made.

I believe that in order to truly help our clients, we must combine traditional counseling methods with coaching techniques. Many clinicians express to me the hesitancy to take on a more coaching role out of fear of taking on more liability with these clients. What I tell these clinicians is that if you are working hard to maintain proper boundaries and being careful to maintain confidentiality and proper therapeutic boundaries, then rarely could anything happen that could raise your liability. It is natural to be cautious about getting in to trouble with the licensing board, but nowhere does it say that we cannot work in the community with the client. As long as we uphold our ethical duties, then it will never be an issue.

Remember, there are significant numbers of untrained and unlicensed "life coaches" working with people in the community. They do not have any formal psychological training and have been making very good livings for the past several years. As professionally educated and trained clinicians, we can do what they do not only better, but also provide more integrated psychological help with evidence-based and research-backed techniques. Do not be afraid to get down in the dirt with your clients. You will find whatever hesitancy that you have will go away quickly once you see how much more progress can be made by working with your clients in this manner.

Okay, now that I have said my part, let's start talking about coaching our clients through the next phase of their treatment. At this point in treatment the client is motivated for change and is ready to move in one direction or another. If we have done our jobs correctly, the client should have at least two or three possible career directions to go in. This can be a good and a bad thing at the same time. It is a good thing because they went from having no idea of what they wanted to do to having multiple ideas. It can also be a bad thing because having multiple options brings up several new roadblocks to progress.

The biggest problem is that with many of these clients, there is a hesitancy to make the wrong decision. I have had many clients say to me that out of fear of choosing the wrong career path and wasting time and money, they simply waffle at making a choice and end up being stagnant. The second major issue is just pure indecision—meaning that they simply cannot decide which option is best for them. I think the problem with pure indecision is rooted in the fact that many clients want to know with 100 percent certainty what the best direction is. You will often see this pattern of thinking not only with career choices but also throughout most of their life decisions. What I tell my clients in this situation is that, with the exception of Jennifer Lopez throwing herself at you, rarely will there ever be a decision in life that you will have 100 percent certainty. So what we have to do is analyze all of the pros and cons of any decision and choose the one that makes the most sense.

This is where the real coaching begins with your clients. What I will do is go over every in and out of any particular career choice that we have isolated and then compare them to the other choices. What you will usually notice is that there is a pretty clear choice for what is the best choice for them. With that being said, while I believe coaching takes on a more proactive role in this process than in counseling, I firmly believe that just like in counseling, we do not tell our clients what to do. It is not our place to tell them what decision to make. What is our job in these cases is to simply present the data to them and observe that one choice may have more pros than cons than others.

Most clients will usually see that one career has more advantages than the others and will decide to go in that direction. However, many clients have severe self-doubt, and making a decision to go in one direction will bring about a lot of anxiety. When clients are confronted with anxiety, they will either confront the anxiety or move on or they will run away from the anxiety and avoid. It is at this point where you will begin to incorporate your own counseling theories to help the client through this anxiety. Many times it is rooted in negative beliefs/schemas, but many times the anxiety and self-doubt go much deeper and must be explored with your client. This is why I believe that we are better equipped than life coaches to deal with these issues because life coaches do not have the first clue how to deal with this anxiety or even how to assess how pathological it might be.

In my experience, there is no real way to quantify how much time it will take to move beyond this part of treatment. Some clients move quickly through their decision while others may waffle for a bit and will need some extra counseling and coaching. In some cases where you suspect deeper lying psychological issues (i.e., anxiety, depression, etc.), you may have to take some time to work on those issues before you go back to being proactive and getting back on track.

Once the client has made a final decision on their career path, the real fun begins in your sessions. With a clear destination in hand, we can begin to make a road map with step-by-step way points for them to follow. What I do is take out the following chart and on one end I put the career that they have chosen and on the other end I put down this is the present situation. From there, we simply work forward with all of the necessary steps to get them to where they need to be. Figure 11.1 is a sample blank worksheet:

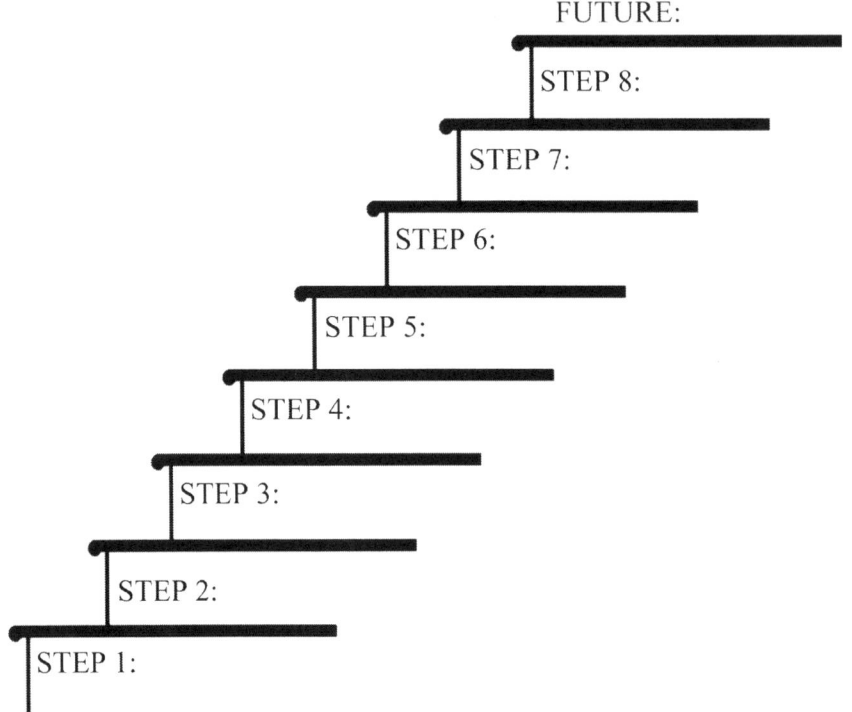

Figure 11.1. Career Path Worksheet.

For example, let's say that we have a client who is currently a freshman at a local community college and they have decided that they want to pursue a career in psychology. The following chart will look like this (see figure 11.2):

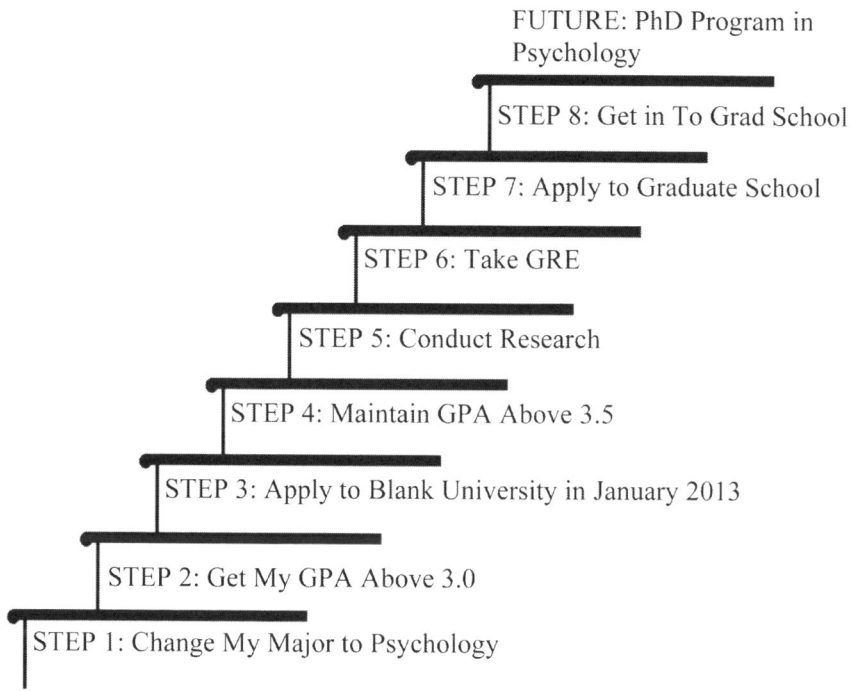

Figure 11.2. Long-Term Plan for Success.

Let me walk you through each step using the above example. What I typically do is start with the very first step and lay out specifically what they have to do to change their major. So many times we assume that the client knows how to do this, so I will literally go online with them and look up the exact procedures for changing their major and exactly who they will need to see to do that. If an appointment has to be made with an advisor, I will usually get on the phone with the client and schedule an appointment. This specific action ensures that the client will follow through on this task.

Another thing to mention is that your client may potentially have problems with social anxiety. More specifically, your client may have fears about confronting their academic advisor, especially if their grades have not been stellar up to that point. I had one client in particular who expressed worry about seeing his advisor for fear that the counselor would "not like me and think that I am a slacker." It is important to discuss these irrational beliefs with the client and even role-play the situation with them.

In extreme cases of failure to launch, I will have one of the licensed counselors in my practice actually meet with the client at their home and actually take them to the school to get their major changed. I particularly enjoy have the luxury of having a life coach at my employ because it allows me to offer a more intensive and comprehensive service to my clients, ensuring that my clients will do the things that they need to.

In the second step, the client has expressed a desire to get a 3.0 GPA which is the typical GPA that is required to transfer to a major university. What I typically do is engage the client on their study habits and what they have typically done in the past. I will go over everything from how often they go to school, how they take notes, how they study, how they do their homework, how they organize their notebooks, and their study schedule.

After ascertaining where the majority of their academic problems are, I coach the client on improving in those areas. I will often help the client by teaching them better study habits, how to do homework more efficiently, how to schedule their time better, how to write papers, and so forth. Usually with some minor coaching, they will be able to improve their academic performance greatly. However, you will also find that many of your clients have either a previous diagnosis of ADHD and learning disabilities or will display several symptoms of ADHD and learning disability and have never been formally diagnosed or treated.

For cases like this, I will typically do some ADHD assessments to gather some additional clinical information. In more severe cases, I will often send them with the testing data to a psychiatrist for medication management or an educational psychologist for a full-battery assessment to determine what learning disabilities they might have. You would be amazed at how many young adults have slipped through the cracks and have never been tested for any type of learning disability or attention difficulties.

Once you can rule out any psychological reasons for their academic problems or that they have been formally treated for said problems, we can begin to sit back and see how the client responds to the coaching. If the client has internalized the coaching and is motivated for change, the client should start doing much better in school and be rather self-sustaining with their academics. Some students made need some cheerleading along the way. I have many clients who really do not need any additional coaching but come in once per month just because they like the accountability of working with somebody.

With the latter steps in this particular example, the client should be launched by now and be able to do all of the later steps without any additional help. With most plans extending out over several years, refresher sessions are recommended just to make sure they continue their progress or I tell clients just to give me a call if they hit a roadblock and need some additional help.

In the above example, the client laid out a long-term plan for success. But what about a client with more simple and short-term goals? Many parents will bring their child in to my office with very little expectations for their child. In many of these cases, you will see some underlying psychological problems such as Asperger's syndrome, personality disorders, recent substance abuse problems, and so forth. In these cases, setting simple short-term goals will be the best option. This allows us to realistically meet the client where they are at while also giving them small successes that will help build their confidence to tackle bigger goals. Let's take a look at how we would work with a small goal (see figure 11.3):

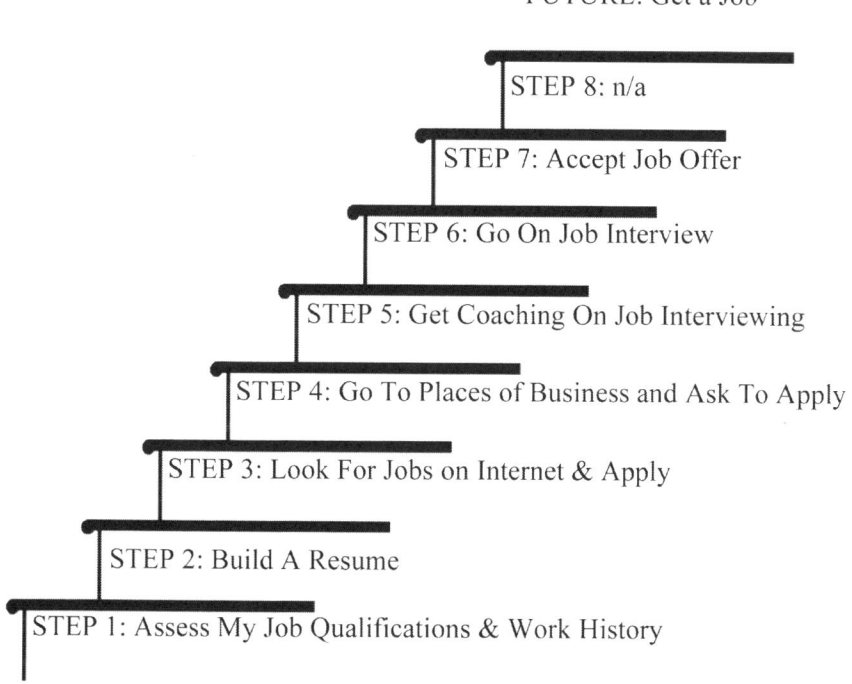

Figure 11.3. Short-Term Plan for Success.

In this particular example, the very first place that I start with my clients is to get their full job history. Many of my clients have never worked a job in their life, so I will write down whatever volunteer jobs or church positions that they have held. This is an important step because the job market is so competitive now that it is a waste of time for our clients to apply for jobs that they have no experience with. Plus it is an easier transition to start a job where you have some experience with.

After getting a good idea of their work history, I will sit down with the client in my office and either update their resumé or build a new one from scratch. You would be amazed at how many employers are requiring resumés, even for the most menial of jobs. I try to make this as collaborative as possible, getting specific with what their skills are and what they have accomplished in their career.

The most difficult step is the actual job search and application process. Many of the clients that I have worked with have an aversion to work and will find every reason in the book to not apply for a job. Despite their reservations, we have to try to find a middle ground with them. I usually go on a particular job-posting website, and we will try out different keywords that we generate from their previous work experience. I read each job posting aloud to them, and we make a list of all the jobs that they qualify for and/or the jobs that are appealing to them.

One thing that can come up with clients who have very little self-esteem is the claim that they do not qualify for a particular job. You would be surprised at how our clients will undersell themselves and will just assume that the company will not want them. What I usually tell my clients is that you have everything to gain by applying to a job and nothing to lose by applying to a job. Let the company decide for you whether or not you qualify, do not make that decision for them.

Usually with a bit of coaxing, I can get most of my clients to agree on several different jobs. With the clients that I trust to get it done, I will send them home with a list of jobs to apply to. However, there are going to be several clients that you know ahead of time that will come in the next session with not a single job applied for. In cases like this, I will literally use our session time to apply to as many jobs as we can. This will ensure that the client is applying to the jobs.

After we have exhausted every online lead, I will then have my clients go to places of business in their community and introduce themselves and ask if they could fill out a job application. I do this for several reasons. First, I think it is a great way to do in-vivo exposure therapy for my clients with social anxiety. Second, many small businesses do not have applications online, and they only accept applications in person. Lastly, so many people apply online for jobs, and many of them will never see the light of day by a hiring manager. If a client goes in personally, then there is an opportunity to make an impression, and the store manager can pull the application to make sure the person will get an interview.

Once again, in some cases clients will be hesitant or anxious about going in to stores by themselves. In these cases, I will send one of my life coaches out with the client and help coach them through their anxiety, plus it ensures that we will get the client out of the house and in to the job hunt.

After a week or so, the client should start getting calls from potential employers for job interviews. Since many of our clients have rarely worked or suffer from intense anxiety, it is extremely beneficial to coach them on job interview skills. Since I have experience with executive assessment, I will coach my clients on what employers are looking for and go over possible interview questions that they will likely see. I often will have one of my other counselors conduct mock interviews to ensure that I can put them into a novel situation that will induce anxiety that they will feel in a real interview. After getting feedback from the mock interviews, we take that feedback and work on the areas in which they are not as strong in.

At this point the process is largely out of our hands, and we hope that the client has been coached well and does well in the interview. The only other place where you can help the client is if they have multiple job offers and you can help them decide which job is for them.

As you can see in the two examples that I provided, we simply help our clients set a goal for themselves, and we gather all the necessary information so we can ascertain what steps they need to take and how to coach them through each step. Each client will be different, and it will take your clinical judgment to determine how involved you will get in the process.

I have had several conversations with clinicians that ask me if I feel as though coaching, especially intensive coaching will hurt the client in the long run. They explain that they fear that the coaching will act more like a crutch for the client and when you start to back off, they will return to their original self. My answer to their concerns is that it is a valid concern and that we have to be careful to not act as a crutch to our clients. That is why it is so important to have an accurate assessment of your client and their underlying psychological issues. I always lean toward having the client do as much on their own as possible, but in some cases they simply need some extra help, motivation, and external pressure to get things done.

There will be some clients who display several avoidant and dependent personality characteristics, and you will have to walk a fine line with coaching them because they are used to people doing everything for them and they can become dependent on the extra help. When providing intensive coaching with these clients, always use the coaching as means to get some initial forward progress, but quickly taper off and put more responsibility on them.

At this point in treatment, we have literally thrown everything in our tool bags as clinicians to get the client internally motivated to make changes in their lives. We will have helped them decide what their personal goals are as well as laid out a step-by-step plan for them to accomplish their goal. We even will have coached them along the entire way just to make sure they have all of the needed along the way. If at this point we are unable to get the client to make progress on their own, then it is time to involve the family and determine what kind of external pressure we will apply.

As I stated in the beginning of this section, our first choice is to have the client launch themselves into the future, but if they are unable or unwilling, then we have to involve the family and begin the difficult process of having them draw a line in the sand. The proceeding chapters will walk you through the process of working with the family and training them to be the agents of change.

Chapter Twelve

Empowering the Family

Being a therapist is an interesting job because we tend to view people on many different levels. When I have parents sitting across from me saying how worried they are about their child and how powerless they feel to help them, I generally feel their pain and empathize with them. Imagine what it would be like to raise your child for eighteen years and put so much time, energy, and resources into them, hoping that you gave your child everything they need to be happy, successful, and have a family of their own one day. Then they have the realization that all of their effort has resulted in an adult child who has no desire to succeed in life.

By the time parents come in to my office, they are battle weary and completely exhausted from trying to fix the problem on their own. The number one statement that I get from parents is "Michael, we feel totally powerless to do anything about the situation." While I can empathize with their pain, the therapist in me sees the situation for what it is, often eliciting the automatic thought of "What do you mean you have no power to change the situation, you are the one holding all of the cards."

Whether it's the parents' own enabling behaviors or great manipulation by the child, parents seem totally oblivious to the fact that they have all of the power in the system. They literally do not see that they are holding all of the cards, and they can easily change the game by actually using the power that they have. In other families where there is a high level of enabling, the parents see the power that they have; they just simply do not want to exercise it over the anxiety that it will create in them.

Whether a parent wants to exercise their power or not, they have been put in to a position by their child at this point to where they really have no choice. If I am having a conversation with a parent about assessing what their power is and how to use it, then that means we have tried internally motivating their child and it has failed. If they want their child to have a chance at being a successful adult, then this is their last and only option.

The process of getting this phase of treatment started is very tricky because the adult child is our client, and unless we have permission to speak with the parents, then the manner in which we begin this process is tricky. What I learned is that while you are working with the client individually, you should start planting seeds of what is to come if they are unable to motivate themselves and start progressing in life. What I usually tell my clients is the following:

> *I know your motivation is not the greatest and that it is difficult for you to get certain things accomplished. But I think we have to realize what the score is here. If you are in my office, that means mom and dad are tired of this whole thing and are willing to do anything to get you motivated. In my experience, 90 percent of parents are willing to see if I can get you to make progress on your own terms but will only give you a short amount of time before they decide to force your hand. Most parents will give you two months to make progress before they start drawing lines in the sand and start giving ultimatums. If you feel as though it's tough to do it now, can you imagine the stress of having a date where unless you have a job or are enrolled in school, you have to move out of the house? Honestly, your parents are the ones who called me in the beginning to set this thing up, and I heard it in their voices. They are done with it all, and I can pretty much predict they will make an ultimatum eventually. So really, you are left with a choice of doing it now on your terms or doing it later under a time frame and under their terms.*

By saying this, I have prepared the client for this phase of treatment. It will not be a surprise to them, and it actually gives you some leeway to say that I told you this was going to happen. Furthermore, even though secretly it is really your idea to get mom and dad to set an ultimatum, it takes the blame off of you and puts it on mom and dad, thus preserving your relationship with the client.

In my experience, I typically see this phase of treatment coming a mile away. Usually after six weeks or so, you will get a good idea of whether or not your client is making progress. When you begin to get the idea that your client is not making progress, there are two different ways to get the parents involved in counseling.

In a family system that is heavy on enabling, some parents will simply let things go on forever. In these cases, I usually ask the client for permission to speak with their parents so that I can get their view of the problem. Some clients will be wary of this move, and I will tell them that since they are having so much conflict with their parents, it would be helpful to hear their side of the story so that I can figure out what is going on and to see what I can do to make things better at home.

Many clients are hesitant to talk with their parents and actually think it's a good idea so I can "talk" with them and set the score straight. Ironically this move can strengthen your relationship with the client because it looks like you are sticking up for them.

After getting permission to speak with the parents, I will call them and ask them how they feel as though things are going. If I am making this call, I already know that things are not good, but I really want to hear what the parents have to say. I lead off with saying that I cannot divulge anything about what I and their child speak about in counseling but would like to get their view of the problem and to gauge where they are at as far as patience. Most parents will be very receptive to this and will be open to sitting down with you to give you any information that you need.

The second way that this situation will progress is when after about the same amount of time, you will get a phone call from a parent. It usually starts off with something like "I don't want my son/daughter to know that I am calling, but I feel as though you needed to understand what is going on at home with them." Most parents will respect client-patient confidentiality, but I tell them right off the bat that I won't talk about what I discussed with their child during sessions.

At this point I completely understand that the parents have reached the end of their rope and it is time to bring the family in to speak with me. In the majority of cases, I do not tell my clients that their parents will be coming in, and I only sit down and speak with the parents alone. That way the parents can speak freely without worrying about the reaction that their child would have to what they have to say.

These meetings are usually pretty interesting because you never really know what is going to come out of the parents' mouths. Some parents will express anxiety and concern over their child, often crying about their lack of progress and their fear for their future. I have some parents that come in and start dropping f-bombs all over my office and saying how they feel taken advantage of by their child.

Regardless of their reactions, we have to bring the family together to work the problem. Many times parents will bicker at each other and rehash every mistake that the other has made in the past. Many times I will strongly interrupt them and say that the past really does not matter at this point. We cannot go back and change what happened. All we have the power to do is make changes from this point going forward and that is exactly what we are going to do.

The most important thing that you have to remember during these family sessions is to stay as structured as humanly possible. In most cases, you are dealing with a dysfunctional family system with much of the dysfunction being at the spousal level. What could be a productive session can easily turn in to a sparring match between the parents, and the session will be lost to digression after digression.

To help combat this, I usually have a set format that I follow, and I tend to be very directive in the sessions with the parents. I will give the parents a bit of leeway, but if I feel as though they are beginning to digress, I will usually redirect them very quickly.

The first question that I ask parents is telling me when the problems began. I like this question because knowing when the problems began will help you define the problem. If the parents say that this has been a problem since he was a young child, then it helps you understand that this has been a struggle for a very long time and that the problem is very much something developmental with the child as well as a problem with how the family system adapted to the problem. If it has been a problem since he was a young child, I will ask how the problem developed and what they did along the way to correct the problem. This is also great information to have because it gives you insight into how involved the parents were in raising him and it gives you data about what has worked and what has not worked in the past. Lastly, if the parents have been dealing with this for a long time, they are exhausted at this point in time, and it helps you empathize that many parents on the inside may want to cut and run from the problem or throw money at it.

If the parents say that this problem developed more recently such as in high school or in the first years of college, this lets me know that this is less a developmental issue and more based on outside factors such as their friends, social habits, and parenting habits. In cases such as this, you will see that the parents did not do a good job of punishing the child and setting boundaries with them. They made attempts to punish them but at the same time did not let them feel the full consequences of their actions. They would lay boundaries but would not follow through on them. The list is endless.

The next question that I ask parents is what their goals are for their child and for our work together. This is a great question as well because it gives me information about how lofty, realistic, or weak their goals are for their child. In an enabling family system, many families have very weak goals for their child. For example, I had a family in my office whose son was a recovering heroin addict who likely had mild Asperger's syndrome as well. Despite the problems that he had, he was fairly high functioning and was capable of working, going to school, and living on his own. His mother was an anxious individual who was scared about her son being pushed too hard and going back to using drugs again or having a mental break down. When I asked her what her goals were for her child, she said that she just wanted him to be healthy and safe. She balked at her husband's desire to get a job and go to school and even began crying when she expressed her fears that he was not able to do that. She was happy with him just coming to therapy and exercising every day.

With this family system, the mother's own anxiety about her son's safety made her lowball what she expected out of him. She was putting her anxiety off on her child, and as a result, her goals were too low for him and, ergo, he only did the bare minimum. In cases such as this, it is our job to help the parent understand what their son or daughter is capable of doing. In the above example, I was rather blunt with the mother and told her that they were paying me to assess their child and they needed to trust me to know what their child can and cannot do.

In other cases, you will have parents that will set the bar way too high for their child. For example, I had a family in my office whose son was a promising 4.0 GPA student in high school and was enrolled in a prestigious computer science program at a private university. The client started experiencing depression, anxiety, and home sickness, eventually failing his classes and taking a temporary medical leave from school for the spring. When the client was presented for counseling, he was barely functioning, and just getting out of bed was a chore for him. The initial goals that we set were just getting a job and slowly figuring out what the client wanted to do about college in the fall. As counseling progressed, more problems came out, and it was apparent that he had several personality issues as well as a codependent relationship that was really the main reason he came home from school.

After a month, the client had a job and was taking summer school classes at a local community college. After two months, the parents requested a meeting and said that they wanted him back at school in the fall, wanted him to break up with his girlfriend, play less video games, volunteer at school, and act more enthusiastic. I told the parents that their expectations, while desirable, were too lofty and that he met every goal that they initially requested of him. The mother of the client was visibly anxious and was catastrophizing that the girlfriend was going to hold him back and he would never go back to school; ergo, he would be a bum. The parents refused to listen to my reasoning, and they gave the child an ultimatum to break up with the girlfriend or move out. The client chose to move out, and the parents lost any leverage or power that they had over the situation.

This situation is very common, and you will be profoundly frustrated by these parental systems. As I said in early chapters, a parent's own anxiety is a huge contributor to the failure-to-launch child, and you will see it play out in your office. That is why asking them what their goals are for their child is such a powerful question; it will bring out the dysfunctional family dynamics.

After discussing the parents' goals for their child, I will usually spend a good chunk of the session managing the parents' expectations about what are realistic goals for their child. One thing to note here is that in many cases, one parent will want one thing and the other will want something else. A huge part of our job is to get mom and dad on the same page. One thing that has helped me bring parents together is to tell them that it is not your job to see things eye-to-eye, but it is your job to find a middle ground here. I try to hear each parent's concerns, express understanding, empathy, and so forth. I reflect back what they say but always redirect them to a more realistic goal set and a goal set that is a good middle ground that each parent can agree upon.

After we have an agreed upon set of goals for the parents, I conduct what I call a power analysis with the parent. When parents come in to our office, they feel powerless over the situation because their child is an adult. You will hear the child throw this at the parents, that they cannot make him do anything. But just because a child is an adult does not mean that the parents are powerless to do anything. The truth of the matter is that they have a ton of power over the situation.

What I do is ask the parents what they do to help support their child. You will get a range of answers but here are the top answers that I hear from parents:

1. Pay for their rent.
2. Allow them to stay rent free at home.
3. Pay for their car and insurance.
4. Pay for cell phone.
5. Provide a free credit card.
6. Give them money when they need it.
7. Pay for college.
8. Pay for groceries.

When you look at this list, it is quite apparent that if you took away a lot of these things, a person really would not be able to support themselves, would they? When I read over the list of items, I ask the parents what would happen if they took away these things. Most parents will say that the child could not function as their life currently stands and would have to make a life change. When you reframe all of these items as power, the parents all of a sudden realize that they do hold most of the cards in the situation; all they have to do is play their cards. This step will empower the parent more than any other step.

But what if a child is struggling with substance abuse or mental health issues and the parents really do not support the child at all? If we are dealing with a substance abuse problem, I usually will help guide the parents on an intervention for the child. In many cases you can easily help the parents do an intervention on their own, but in extreme cases, I do have the option of bringing in a trained interventionist to mediate the intervention.

In cases of a child struggling with mental health issues such as severe depression, suicidal ideations, and thought disturbances, the parents' options become a bit more limited depended on state/city laws, insurance coverage, and so forth. I instruct most parents that if their child is threatening themselves or others, then they always have the option of calling the police and having them come out to the home to determine if they have enough evidence to file a mental illness warrant and take the child to the hospital. Each state or city has different laws regarding mental illness warrants, and you should check the laws in the state that you practice in. For those of you unfamiliar with mental illness warrants, they allow the police to not "arrest" the client but rather have them put into protective custody so that they can be taken to a hospital for evaluation. If the client meets criteria, a hospital can hold the client for up to seventy-two hours against their will.

With the power in hand, I ask them how far they are willing to go to get their child launched into the future. This question will also ellicit important data because it will let you know if the parents are ready to make changes of their own. In an enabling family system, you will find that one parent is not willing to do what is necessary to get their child launched. For example, I posed this question to the family of a former drug abuser and asked what they were willing to do to get their child launched. The father said that if by a certain date the boy had not gotten a job, then he wanted to kick him out of the house. The mother started crying and said that she could not kick her child out of the house because he was innovative; he would start selling drugs and would get killed in a drug deal.

It is at this point where the enabling family dynamic will rear its head. Despite the problems that their child's behavior causes on the family, the dysfunction serves a purpose. Many times the child's problems are subconsciously aimed at distracting the parents from their own problems in their lives. When we ask the parents what actions they are willing to take to change the system, you will find that many parents do not have the ego-strength to make those changes on their own.

What you also see in this example is a very common occurrence—one parent willing to go further than the other. This is very common and in fact is probably more common than not. My job is not to say if one parent is more right than the other, but rather to help them determine which boundary is most likely to get the desired change.

When we really look at the boundaries that a parent must set with their child, they come in two different categories. The first category is what I consider basic boundaries, which can include making the child pay rent, pay for their own schooling, drug testing, paying for other bills on their own, and so forth. The second level is what I consider the nuclear option boundaries, which typically include making the child move out of the house, pulling all financial support, drug treatment, mental health treatment, and cutting off communication.

Having a good idea of the problem will help you guide your parents on what boundaries to set because sometimes going with the nuclear option right off that bat with a child whose behaviors do not warrant a nuclear response can cause more problems than it will solve. To help gauge how much of their power they should exercise, I consider the following criteria:

1. Have they tried setting expectations/boundaries in the past?
2. If they did set expectations/boundaries, did they follow through with the consequences when the child did not hold up to their end of the bargain?
3. Are their severe mental health problems evident in the child?
4. If the child has never had expectations put on their behavior in the past, do you think basic boundaries will work if the parents follow through?

If the parents have never set boundaries or had expectations for their children in the past, then why would you choose nuclear options when the basic options have never been tried? In these cases, get the parents to agree to basic options first before using the big guns. Sometimes parents will say that we have tried having written out expectations/boundaries in the past and they didn't work. Probe the parents on this statement because many times you will find out that while they had expectations, they never followed through with the consequences. If they never enforced the consequences, then they never really had a chance to see if boundaries would work.

What if the client has severe mental health problems? I have several clients with pervasive developmental disorders such as Asperger's syndrome or thought disorders such as schizophrenia. When you have clients with the impairment of psychological problems, they very well may not be able to fully support themselves. In one case, a parent went against my advice and decided to kick their Asperger's syndrome son out of the house because he would not get a job. Their child literally sat on the curb all night and did not go anywhere for two days. Power is a great thing to have, but we are looking to exercise power that will promote change, not keep them in the same place.

Lastly, just use your clinical judgment and your knowledge of the client's history. If you feel as though the nuclear options are what they need, go ahead and recommend that. But if you feel as though basic boundaries will work, then do not be afraid to recommend those even if the parents want to go nuclear.

At this point, you should have both parents on the same page, and it is time to move on to the next stage of treatment.

IV

It's Now Up to the Family

Chapter Thirteen

Preparing for Launch

After meeting with the parents for the initial session, we now have a clear direction to start moving in. If you did your job right, you should have the following information:

1. What the parents are specifically expecting out of the child.
2. What power the parents hold over the child.
3. How far the parents are willing to go to get their child progressing in life.
4. Having an agreed upon consensus among the power holders in the family.

The above information is invaluable to the process, but it is by no means a finished product. We simply have an informal agreement between the parents and a rough outline for what the plan is going to be.

A mistake that parents have commonly made in the past was to informally present their expectations to their child without putting anything in writing. This is a huge error because parents will often forget the fine details of their expectations and will become confused as to when they should follow-through with consequences. Furthermore, a child will often try to manipulate the parents with comments such as, "Well, you never told me I couldn't do that" or "I did not know I couldn't do that."

To make sure that a child knows what is expected of them and when the parents should enforce a consequence, a formal contract needs to be drawn up. There are a million different ways to draw up a contract and you can get really cute with it, but I find that the simpler the contract, the better it is for everybody to understand and enforce.

The contract-making process can be an arduous process; just ask any lawyer. What I try to do is simplify the process as much as possible and expedite it as quickly as possible. After the initial session with the parents, I have them come in for a second contract negotiation meeting where we finalize every detail.

The first step in the contract negotiation phase of the contract phase is negotiating the exact terms of the contract or what I would like to call specificity. At this point we only have rough expectations from the parents and the furthest that they are willing to go to get their child launched. We need to get specific about these details because the contract will fall apart from both sides if the child has no idea what exactly is expected of them and what will happen if they don't meet those expectations.

The first area where we need more specificity is the exact expectations of the parent. As I said earlier, if you do not get specific, it will be impossible to enforce regularly and their child will run them around in circles saying things like "That is not in the contract." So we need to make sure every contingency and loophole is taken care off in the wording of the contract.

So let's take a look at some common expectations that parents have given me in the past and go through the process of getting more specific. One of the most common expectations is parents asking their child to get a job. If you simply tell a child to get a job, a child can look forever and simply tell mom and dad, "Well . . . I have been looking." Or there is my personal favorite, the child will get a job but they will only be working five hours per week. It's very easy for the child to say, "You told me to get a job and now I have one."

So I always tell parents that we have to get very specific with what "getting a job" means. I ask them the following questions:

1. How many hours per week do you want them working?
2. What kind of job do you want them working at?
3. What is the exact date you want them to be working by?
4. What are the requirements if he gets fired (i.e., how long does he have to find another job)?
5. During the application process, how many applications do you want them filling out each day?
6. If they do not have a job by that date, what will the consequence be?

This information will let the child know exactly what the parents mean by getting a job and leaves nothing up to interpretation. They also understand that there is an exact date that they have to do this by, and if they do not meet the expectations by that date, they know exactly what the consequence is going to be. This puts external pressure on the client, and they have to make an internal choice of doing what their parents want them to do or take the consequence that they have laid out.

It is important to note that the consequence must be strong enough to make them prefer to get a job. These kids do not want to work, and we must present them with an option that is even less desirable than getting a job. It should come down to choosing the lesser of two evils. If the consequence is not less desirable than the expectation, then they will rather take the consequence. The analogy that I use with parents is:

"Imagine that we are a demolition company and we need to blow up a building. Let's say it will take 100 tons of TNT to blow up the building. If we use 95 tons, we will get a big explosion, but it will not take the building down. We have to use 100 tons or more. But this is also a controlled demolition so if we use 200 tons of TNT, then we will blow up the entire city block along with the building."

Using the work example from above, the specifics could look something like this:

1. John has to get a part-time job working no less than twenty hours per week.
2. John must have a job and have a start date no later than September 1.
3. If John does not have a job by September 1, then the following consequences will be enacted (basic consequences) (*nuclear consequences*):

a. All financial support will be pulled from mom and dad.
b. You will turn in your cell phone and all credit cards.
c. You have to pay for all of your bills and spending money.
d. *You will turn over your keys to your car.*
e. *You must move out of the house by September 2.*
f. *You will not have any support from your parents and will be self-sufficient for everything.*

It is important to discuss the economy right now because it is more difficult to find a job right now than it has been in the past. If a parent is asking that a child get a full-time forty-hours-per-week job, they may have to find some flexibility with that request because many companies are only hiring part-time or temporary employees so that they do not have to give them benefits. Also, it is more difficult for college-aged people to get a job because so many adults are out of work. Companies prefer to hire an adult because they perceive them as being more reliable and will not leave in the fall or spring for school.

With those facts in mind, it may take longer for a client to get a job, and we must account for that in the contract. We also have to protect the parents from their child using this data to prolong their job search. I have had several clients who had been looking for a job for over a month and could not find a job. When their parents would get mad at them for still being unemployed, they would fire back that they were applying for jobs and it was not their fault for not getting hired. When I would probe at how many jobs they were applying to a day, many times it would be two or three.

So we have to account for the child doing just enough to say that they are applying to a job. The easy way around this is to include language similar to the following:

1. During the job application process, you must made a good faith effort to attain employment. You must apply to ten jobs per day and be able to show proof (e-mail confirmations or a log of where you applied to and when).
2. If you are not applying to the minimum job application requirement, then it will be considered that you are not looking for a job and you will have to move out of the house by September 2.
3. If you are applying to the minimum number of jobs and are still unemployed by September 1, then you must find a volunteer position by October 1 where you will work no less than twenty hours per week.

In extreme cases where the child has bad motivational issues, I will include the following language to ensure that their full-time job is to find a job:

1. During the job application period, your full-time job will be to find a job. You must be dressed professionally every weekday morning and be out of the house by 9:00 a.m. and will not be allowed to come home until 5:00 p.m. The doors will be locked and will not be unlocked until we return home from work at 5:00 p.m.
2. You must provide a log sheet of the jobs that you applied to and what else you did during your day to help you attain a job.

I find that having to go this far is a rare move, but you will find that clients with spectrum disorders and other severe mental health issues may need this extra level of requirements.

Another expectation that can get convoluted is college. Many parents want their children to go to school, but many children either do not want to go to school or find it difficult to motivate themselves to do well in school. Some of my clients feel an entitlement that their parents will pay for their schooling but have not shown any evidence to their parents that they are worth the financial investment of school. This is where a contract can really help a parent because regardless of the situation, you can word a contract to cover every contingency.

For example, I had a family where the client really wanted to go to school, but the family was hesitant because he had either failed out or withdrawn from school every time previously. The client would get angry at his parents for not supporting his dreams, and the family was adamant about not throwing away good money after bad results. We came to an agreement that protected the parents but also gave the client an opportunity to go to school and build up their trust again. Here is how the contract was worded:

1. Starting fall semester, Bobby will attend classes on a full-time basis (fifteen credit hours) at Blank Community College.
2. Bobby will take out temporary student loans to cover his school tuition for books.
3. At the conclusion of the semester, Bobby's parents will reimburse college tuition and books for every class that earns a grade higher than a B.
4. For every class with a grade C or lower, Bobby will have to repay all the costs associated with that class on his own.

What we did in this contract was protect the parents from losing any more money. The temporary loans that most community colleges offer go into the student's name, unlike federal student loans where the parents need to co-sign. Bobby gets the opportunity to go back to school, and at the same time, we apply pressure on him to perform or he is going to be out his own money instead of his parents.

I have also seen several situations where the client does not want to go to school or work. In situations like this, parents will often make an ultimatum where the clients either go to school full-time, work full-time, or go to school part-time and work part-time. Any way you look at it, we can account for these issues in a contract as well. I had this very problem with a family that I worked with earlier this year, and this is the contract wording that we came up with:

To continue living in our home and receiving financial support, the following conditions must be met:

1. Adam must be enrolled in school full-time (fifteen credit) hours at blank community college.
2. If Adam chooses to go to school part-time, he must take at least six credit hours of classes and work a part-time job working no less than twenty hours per week.
3. If Adam chooses to not to go school at all, then he must work a full-time job (forty hours per week).
4. If Adam is not enrolled in classes nor has a job by September 1, then he must move out of the home and his parents will pull all financial support.

This is why contracts are so great, we can literally contract for anything, just as long as we are specific as to what the expectations are and what will happen if the client does not follow through.

I get many questions from parents about how to handle contracting with substance abuse and mental health issues. With substance abuse issues, there are only a few options that are available to parents. Pure and simple, if a parent is going to have a child live in their home and support them, than they cannot allow their child to use any substances.

I have had several parents ask me if it was okay to let the client smoke pot, often giving me the reason that "at least they aren't using meth anymore." I even had one parent say to me after I confronted her about allowing her son to use heroin "well he is only snorting it, at least he is not shooting it." If a parent allows their child's drug use to continue and fully support them, then they are enabling their drug use. The following is an excerpt from a contract that I worked on with a family whose son had a heroin problem.

To continue living in our home with the full support of your parents, the following conditions must be met:

1. Greg must be drug free while living in our home and will be subject to random drug testing.

2. If Greg tests positive for any substance or is found in possession of any substance, the following actions will be taken:

   a. Greg must accept that he has a drug problem and admit himself into a drug rehabilitation program.
   b. If Greg refuses to go into a treatment program, then he must pick up his belongings and leave the house immediately.
   c. If Greg refuses to go into a treatment program, then he will not receive any support from his family.
   d. Treatment will always be an option, so if he agrees to treatment at a later time, he will receive the support of the family.

3. If Greg refuses a drug test at any point, then it will be treated as a positive drug result and the above actions will be taken.

4. Greg must attend no less than three NA meetings per week and attend weekly counseling sessions.

As you can see in the above example, we tried to account for every possible outcome for the family. We structured the contract to make sure that they were trying to help their son out but also made it clear that there was no room for error and they were not going to enable the problem.

The last example that I will go over is the issue of mental health problems and behavior. This is by far the most difficult problem to contract for. The reason is because with the other problems, meeting expectations can easily be quantified by grades, positive drug tests, getting a job, and so forth. But when we are talking about behavior such as anger, disrespect, poor boundaries, and so forth, they can be defined differently. For example, you can have a parent saying that their son was angry and disrespectful to them, but the child will come back saying that his tone was not angry and that the parents are being too sensitive.

When we write a contract with expectations for behavior, we try to be as specific as possible with what behaviors are not tolerated. Furthermore, we try to make a point to say that it will not be one event that will signify noncompliance but rather looking at the overall pattern of behavior over a set period of time. The child may not like it, but it's what the parents view as disrespectful or unacceptable behaviors, not the clients. Here is an example from one of my clients:

To continue living in our home with the full support of your parents, the following conditions must be met:

1. Tom must show respect to his parents and other family members, refraining from the following behaviors:

    a. Cursing at other family members
    b. Degrading or negative comments directed at other family members
    c. Not talking back or making excuses when asked to do something by your parents
    d. No yelling at anybody in the family
    e. Respecting the property of other family members

2. Tom must improve his ability to manage his emotions and refrain from the following behaviors:

    a. Anger outbursts such as breaking household items, punching walls/doors
    b. Threatening comments directed at other family members
    c. Yelling or screaming obscenities

3. If at any time Tom physically threatens his life or anybody in the family, then the following action will be taken:

    a. The police will be called, and they will be instructed that you have a mental health problem and you have made threats to yourself and/or other people.

4. Tom must attend weekly counseling sessions and take any prescribed medication.

5. The length of this contract is thirty days, and all behaviors will be judged by your parents. If at the end of the thirty-day contract your behavior has not been judged to have improved, then the following consequence will be enacted:

   a. Tom will not be allowed to live at home and will be forced to move out of the home within a week of the contract expiring.
   b. Tom will not receive any financial support once he moves out of the home.

As you can see in this example, it is difficult to get specific with certain behaviors, and it is also difficult to quantify what is compliance and what is not.

While I laid out individual examples here to illustrate how to contract for the common problems that you will see, the truth is that many of your contracts may include clauses for all of these problems. When we look at the failure-to-launch problem, it usually involves issues with work, school, drugs, behavior, and so forth.

After getting all the necessary information from the parents, I will make a draft of the contract to send to the parents for their revision. This is important because if they want to change the wording, it is much easier to just e-mail the document to them so that they can review it on their own time instead of wasting time in your office haggling over small details. After the wording of the language is agreed upon, you make a final copy of the contract and begin the process of having a family session to present and discuss the contract.

As I stated in earlier in the chapter, the contract does not have to be very fancy or complicated. All that is important is to be clear and concise. Below you will find a sample contract that I drafted for one of my clients:

JOHN DOE CONTRACT

Expectations:

1. Trust

   a. No blatant lies
   b. No half-truths
   c. No white lies
   d. No gross misrepresentations
   e. Being where you say you will be
   f. Being home when you say you will be home

g. Giving it to your parents straight, no matter how bad the truth might be

2. Respect to Parents

   a. No yelling
   b. No name calling or swearing
   c. No anger outbursts
   d. No facetious comments
   e. No passive aggressive behaviors or comments

3. Respect to Home and Possessions

   a. Cars, furniture, dishes
   b. Leaving dirty dishes upstairs
   c. Throwing trash on the floors in the house and in the garage
   d. Leaving the lights on at night and during the day
   e. Leaving the front door unlocked and the garage door and gate open
   f. Take part in pool maintenance; turn the equipment off after use
   g. Refer to "showing" list; do laundry when his hamper is full; don't occupy laundry room for more than thirty-six hours
   h. I will expect $10 per room per day if I have to clean messes left behind

4. Personal Hygiene and Health (including ADHD recommendations)

   a. Shower after work; oral hygiene
   b. Take meds; high protein breakfast; thirty-minute workout three to four times per week; recommended vitamin supplements
   c. Continuing in treatment and making an honest effort to improve yourself

5. Family

   a. Use some of his time off to visit/telephone grandparents
   b. Make an honest effort to improve relationship with family (e.g., take time out of your week to reconnect with family by going to movie, going out to dinner, etc.)

6. Finances

   a. Repayment plan for total amount owed to parents (payment plan to be determined by parents)
   b. Auto insurance

c. Gasoline
   d. Leasing an automobile from us
   e. Cell phone usage
   f. Discuss misc. items: haircut, clothing, convenience groceries
   g. All bills will be transferred into his name and he will bear responsibility (i.e., poor credit, cell phone being turned off, etc.) for non-payment or late payment.

7. Education

   a. John will have the choice of taking the summer semester off and restarting school in the fall.
   b. John will have to pay for his classes up front (self-pay or temporary loan) and will be fully reimbursed for any grades over a B.
   c. When/if he gets his grades back up over a 2.5 GPA, he can transfer to a school of his choice (preferably in the fall).
   d. Once transferring, he will have to pay for his first semester up front (self-pay/temporary loans) and will be reimbursed for anything over a B.
   e. After one semester of all grades over a B, John's parents will start paying for classes up front.

8. His Character Development

   a. We would like to see him begin attending church again and meeting with his mentor.
   b. If he is not attending school, we'd like him to become a volunteer with a nursing home, boys club, church functions, and so forth.

9. Work

   a. Work was initially supposed to be a part-time job and John will work no more than twenty hours per week if he is in school
   b. If you are not in school, you can work up to thrity hours per week and spend additional time volunteering (see character development).
   c. John must have a job by September 1, 2011.

Penalties:

1. Must Agree to Contract and It's Terms

   a. This contract is completely optional, and John does not have to agree to its terms.

b. If you choose not to agree to these terms: (1) Hand over the keys to the house, pack a suitcase, and you will not be permitted to live in the house anymore; (2) your parents will not provide any current financial assistance (i.e., spending money, car insurance, etc.), and will not provide any future funding for college, room and board, books, and so forth; (3) you will still have a relationship with your parents and can visit with everybody, rather any type of financial relationship will be terminated.
c. If you do not agree to the terms of the contract and decide to live independently, you will have to live independently for a minimum period of six months before you will be allowed to revisit the terms of the contract and enter into a new agreement.

2. *Length of Contract*

   a. The length of the contract runs through September 1, 2011.
   b. Progress will be evaluated by John's parents, and they will determine if John has been meeting the above criteria.
   c. If the criteria have not been met by the above date, John's parents will invoke the following measures: (1) John will hand over the keys to the house and pack a suitcase and will not be permitted to live in the house anymore; (2) your parents will not provide any current financial assistance (i.e., spending money, car insurance, etc.), and will not provide any future funding for college, room and board, books, and so forth; (3) you will still have a relationship with your parents and can visit with everybody, rather any type of financial relationship will be terminated.
   d. If John's parent determine that he has not met the terms of the agreement and have to invoke clause C, then John will have to live independently for a minimum period of six months before he will be allowed to revisit the terms of the contract and enter into a new agreement.

Agreement:

I, John Doe, Do hereby come to agreement with these terms and will abide by the expectationslaid out in this contract and will accept the consequences of breaking this contract.

_____   _____
Signature   Date   Signature   Date

Table 13.1. John Doe Contract.

One last area of contracting that is important to talk about is discussing what the role of the parents will be. Especially in enabling family systems, the parents will often try too hard to get the child to succeed. For example, a family that I was working with had an overly involved mother. On a daily basis, she would overstep her boundaries to keep tabs on what her son was/was not doing. Here is a list of all the things that his mother was doing:

- Checking his bank account on a daily basis and asking him about everything that he spent
- Going over all of his bills and hounding him to pay things on time so that it wouldn't affect his credit
- Going online to check his grades and ask him about every grade he had or assignments that he missed
- Looking through his e-mails to see if he was doing anything inappropriate
- Keeping a log of what he did and at what time to have evidence that he was not doing what he was supposed to

This is by no means a comprehensive list, but rather just a sample of things that the mother was doing. When you ask parents why they do these things, most parents tell me that if they do not do it, then their child will never do it on their own. What I tell parents is that this is really a self-fulfilling prophecy. Out of an attempt to get their child launched in to the future, they are taking actions that actually keep them where they are at. Most of my clients tell me that when parents take actions like this, it only angers them and makes them more complacent.

When we are developing a contract for situations like this, I try to construct a contract to where every goal is measurable. By doing this, I can tell the parents that they no longer have to police their child anymore because the proof is in the pudding. They will either accomplish the goal or they will not. The consequences will be the ultimate equalizer, and they need to let the contract do its work.

The parents need to back off and let the child either succeed or fail on their own. I had one parent respond to this with "What if they do not pay their rent and they get evicted? This will ruin their credit." My response to that is, "Then it will destroy his credit then, that is not your concern." The only way we learn things in this world is to experience the consequences. If I do not pay my car payment, it will be repossessed. If my car is repossessed, I will learn very quickly that is not a desirable experience and I will be sure to never let it happen again.

While it is easy for us to tell a parent to back off, their anxiety will go through the roof, and it will be difficult for them to not do anything. The purpose of a contract in these situations is to also help draw boundaries for the parents to not cross, in essence keeping them honest as well.

Chapter Fourteen

The Launch Pad

One of my favorite movies growing up was *The Right Stuff*. It was a movie about how the U.S. space program was developed. One of the most powerful moments in the movie was when they were testing the rockets for the first time and the astronauts were watching in horror when one rocket after the other would either blow up at the launch pad or explode and fall to the ground shortly after take-off.

When I am visualizing the process in this book, I very much have those images in my mind. An adult child is very much like a rocket isn't it? They are volatile, explosive, precious cargo, difficult to launch, and part of the future.

I titled this "The Launch Pad" because like a rocket, the child is at the launch pad preparing for their launch. When a rocket is at the launch pad, it is getting refueled, its flight plan is getting finalized and uploaded into the computer, the astronauts are loaded, cargo is installed, and every final system checked is conducted. A rocket needs all of these things to make sure that it not only gets off the launch pad safely, but also knows where to go and how to get there as efficiently as possible.

This is the perfect metaphor for this phase of treatment. We are getting the child/family prepared for launch; giving them everything they need to get there safely and efficiently. As clinicians, we are the flight control team in Houston, and this will be the last real chance to work with the family hands on. Because once the rocket lifts off, it really is in the hands of the astronauts. With our family, once we launch this plan, it really is in the hands of the client/family.

The process of presenting a contract to a client is a tricky process. Even though we are calling it a contract, it is basically an ultimatum that the parents are giving their child. We can word it any way that we want to, but their child is going to know exactly what the score is.

To help make this process as smooth as possible, it is going to take some smooth reframing on your part. I have tried many different ways to present this information to my client, and the following process is the best that I have come up with.

The first thing that I do is instruct the parents to speak with their child about their unhappiness with the lack of progress and that they are scheduling a family session to air out all of their concerns. I make sure to strategically schedule an individual session with the client after the parents inform them of the family session but before the actual family session takes place.

When the client comes in to my office and informs me of their parents' displeasure with their progress and the request for the family session, I usually say something along the lines of:

> *You know, I am really not all that surprised. This is something that we discussed was a possibility of happening. You know mom and dad were not happy, which is why they brought you in here. If we are being honest, you really haven't made much progress, and I think they believe that if you are not going to do it on your own, then they are going to make you do it. You really do not have much of a choice do you? My advice is to participate in the process. You have lost a lot of your power to do it on your own, and participating with your parents in the process will at least give you some power over the situation. Let's just sit down with them and see what they have to say and we can go from there.*

The client is usually not happy with the situation at all, but when we reframe the situation to them like that, they kind of see that they really have no choice in the matter and do kind of realize that some of this is their own doing. Clients with high levels of narcissism and egocentrism will display much more anger than clients without it, but regardless of their anger, they see that they really have no option.

To help alleviate any perceived alliance with the parents, I tell the client that I will call the parents to set up a family session and reiterate that I will not share anything that we have discussed.

What is extremely important to remember during the initial family session is that you do not present any formal contract at all or even allude to the fact that you already spoke with the parents about making a contract. I know this may walk the fine line with ethics, but to do so does not break any ethical guidelines here. Our job is to help our clients, and sometimes we do things to help our clients that they are not going to like. Think about this action in the same category of hospitalizing a client or sending them to rehab. They do not want to go and they will be angry at you, but you are doing it because you know it is what is best for them and will ultimately help them.

I usually begin the session by saying that I spoke with the parents on the phone and they expressed some of their concerns to me, but what I am hoping for today is to clear the air and have a discussion about your progress and what your parents' concerns are. I make sure to state that it is not my job to take sides here and that just because somebody has an opinion on something, does not mean it is fact. This will help you diffuse tense moments when a parent makes a statement that angers the child, usually eliciting statements such as, "That's not true," "You are wrong," and "You have no idea why I do what I do," and so forth.

When the child and the parents get in to that back and forth, it can derail/sidetrack the process. Simple comments such as "that is just their opinion" or "so from your perspective" can easily redirect the session and get it back on track. I also make sure to structure the session where each person gets a chance to express themselves without being interrupted. This ensures that each person will get a chance to talk/respond to what each person is saying. This also allows you to manage the session better because emotions will flare up and all you have to do to redirect is say, "Let me hear your mom out for a second; you can respond here in a second I promise." It may seem a little too structured, but it really does help you referee the session. Remember, we are dealing with dysfunctional family systems here. They have no idea how to talk and listen to each other. By structuring the session out like this, we are modeling how to listen and respond.

Another thing to be wary of is to manage emotions during the session. Many times during this initial session, it is the parents whom you have to manage the most. While they do their best to remain civil during the process, some parents lose their cool and will hurl insults or use the opportunity to beat their child over their head with everything that they have done wrong. This does nothing but makes the child shut down and prevents any real dialogue from occurring.

When I was just starting out in private practice, these situations were initially difficult for me because I was a young clinician and it was difficult to really take control of a family session where the parents were much older than me. Even for an older clinician, these types of confrontations can be difficult. Regardless of your anxiety about offending anybody, you must take control of the situation. If the family session becomes an emotional beat down or a shouting match, I often interject firmly that this is not helping. I will empathize with the frustration in the room but state that it is not helping and we need to get back on track.

Many times you will have two parents bickering with one another, especially if they have marital issues, are divorced, or one is a step-parent. When you have parents bickering with each other, use a simple redirection such as "It is pointless to go back and blame each other for past actions; we simply cannot go back in time and change it. The only thing that we can do is learn from the past and move forward from this point forward . . . which is why you are here to begin with."

As the parents are going over their list of concerns, I often will keep an eye on the client and watch for any intense reactions. If I see a strong reaction from the client, I will check in with them to make sure that they are okay. While I want them to wait for their turn to speak/respond, it is also important to make sure that they have not shut down and have stopped listening to their parents. If they have a strong reaction, I will make a comment such as, "That's really a good point. I am writing it down, and I will make sure we get to speak about that."

When it is the client's turn to speak, we hope that we can have a civil dialogue, but many times you will get a negative reaction. In my experience, there are three typical negative reactions from the client. One of the most fun things to watch is the "blamer," which is when the client becomes angry at the parents and blames them for every problem that they have. It is fun to watch because you get to see exactly what happens in the home when the parents have tried to get their child to make changes. Clients have to blame the parents for their problems because if they didn't, they would have to look at themselves as the reason for their lack of progress and they do not have the ego-strength to deal with that.

The next reaction is what I call the "denier," which is when the client denies the parents' view of reality and does not think what they are doing is an issue. The denier will often use excuses such as being depressed or anxious as the reasons for their lack of progress and will state that they need "time" to get healthy. My personal favorite statement from the "denier" is "I cannot be pushed right now because I am in a fragile state of mind."

The last reaction that I see is "the shutdown," which is the client literally shutting down and having little or no reaction. This reaction is complex because there can be different reasons for why this happens. In many cases, the client cannot find any rational argument to what the parents said and realizes that their parents are right and there is simply nothing to say. With clients who are depressed and who have several unresolved issues with their parents, they will adopt the "All they want to do is exert their power over me so what can I really do?" stance. In some cases, the client adopts the "I fu& %ing hate you all, and I am not participating at all" mentality—which I typically liken to a four-year-old sitting on the floor with their arms crossed saying, "No, I am not going anywhere!" These clients realize they have little to no power over the situation, so they revert to a childlike defense to maintain some power in the family system.

Regardless of the negative reaction, it is important to empathize with the client and try to get their level of defenses down. The technique that I have found most effective is to just empathize with the client's frustration and reinforce the fact that we know they are upset but this is their one time to be open, honest, and participate in this process. I say something along the lines of "If you blow up or shut down, you are giving up what little power you have over the situation. If mom and dad are here, then they have reached the end of their line. If you choose not to participate in the process, they are going to choose a path for you without any of your feedback."

Usually after some careful crisis management, the client will calm down and they will begrudgingly participate in the process. Just be weary that just like a fire that has been put out, it can flare up very easily. So be cognizant of that and deescalate any problems quickly.

If we have worked our magic enough, we can have a civil conversation with the client where they can calmly give their reactions to the parents. If they have a differing view, we can discuss why they view things so differently and maybe come to some sort of common ground. If things go well, we can also get an honest dialogue about acknowledging that their parents have several good points about what the client really does need to improve upon.

If we can progress to the client acknowledging that they need to improve in certain areas, we can then engage in an honest conversation about why those things have not happened and what they need to do to make progress in those areas. This is a powerful moment in counseling because if the client has these insights, it builds positive collateral with the parents.

This is very important because when it is the client's turn to speak, many times they have feedback to the parents that might be critical, but actually very accurate. Some parents are way too involved, negative, critical, and anxious, and so forth. If the client is acknowledging his own crap, it makes any constructive feedback that he has to his parents more believable, rather than being defensive or blaming.

What this also does is help the client buy in to the process even more because it doesn't mean that we are doing a family session just to tell him what he is doing wrong; it is about the family being there together to figure out what each person is doing wrong and what changes each person needs to make to function better. While we may play up some of the parent's role in the problem to help lower the client's defenses, in reality this is a systemic issue, and everybody is going to have to change.

After everybody has had their chance to talk, I summarize everything that I heard from the family. By doing this, I make sure that I heard everyone correctly, but it also allows me to set the stage for a contract. What I normally say is that I am going to take everything that has been said here today and help draw up a contract. This statement helps my relationship with the client because it is not me coming up with the contract (even though it is my idea), it is rather me simply taking what I heard and organizing it into a formal document. I also use this time to try to reframe a contract as not only a means to help keep the client accountable for progress, but also to help keep the parents accountable as well. Many of my clients have stated that every time they have gone into an agreement with their parents, the parents have never held-up to their end of the bargain. That actually is a fairly accurate statement, as many parents rarely follow through on consequences or rewards.

By going into a contract with the parents through my process, everybody is accountable to me to uphold the contract. So when a client says that they do not trust their parents and asks me what good will a contract do, I simply respond that I cannot attest to what happened in the past because I was not there. Now that I am involved in the process, if they do not hold up to their end of the bargain, then they have to answer to me. I state that if you are doing your job and mom and dad are not, you call me and I will make sure that they make the proper changes.

After summarizing everything that I have heard, I reserve the last ten minutes of the session just to speak with my client alone. I like to do this because it allows me to check in with my client and see what their reaction is to everything. I also do this because they are often upset with the whole situation and get stuck on how unfair it is.

With many of my clients, I often do some work with core mindfulness. One of the principles of core mindfulness is being nonjudgmental. Part of being nonjudgmental is focusing just on the fact and not judging any situation. If a situation sucks, focusing on how bad it sucks will only make a person more upset; plus it does not change the situation at all. We have to learn to radically accept every situation for what it is, no matter how much we don't want to be in certain situations. If your car dies on the highway, kicking the car and cursing doesn't fix the car. To be effective in the situation, we must focus on what will improve the situation, which is walking to a gas station or calling AAA.

I like going over this with my client after the family session because regardless of how angry they are and how unfair they feel the situation is . . . it is what it really is. They cannot change anything about it, so they have a choice to sit there and be angry or they can learn to radically accept the situation and just be part of the process. The sooner they accept the process and just work through the contract, the quicker they will be independent and be able to make their own decisions.

Usually talking with my clients will help them accept the situation for what it is. I tell my clients that I am going to write everything up and we will all meet next week to go over the contract, sign it, and get everything started right then and there.

With the initial family session out of the way, it is time for the actual contract session. What I do is print up copies of the contract for everybody to have and we all sit down together and go over the contract line by line. I not only read what the contract says, but I explain specifically what it means so there is not confusion on anybody's part.

After going through the contract, I ask if anybody has any questions or last-minute objections. If there are none, then I present them with a pen and everybody signs the contract. I keep the signed contract for my files, and each person has a copy of the contract for their own reference.

At this point in time, we have a signed agreement, and it begins the second they step out of my office. Depending on the contract terms, we will schedule another family session in accordance to the time frame set in the contract. If you have done a good job of writing the contract and coaching the parents, then much of the work is out of your hands and is with the family.

The individual work with the client is very important at this phase because every plan that we have constructed in the past individually speaking was before this contract was put in to place. The contract changes the game, and just like before, we cannot assume that the client will know how to plan for this new future on their own.

I spend the next few sessions going over the terms of the contract with the client and charting a new game plan with them. For example, if the parents have placed an ultimatum of getting a job in four weeks' time, our new goal will be getting a job, and we start a new plan like before with the goal of getting a job in four weeks. What is important to remember during this phase of treatment is that the client is under a time crunch to make something happen. If he had to get a job in four weeks, his full-time job right now should be to get a job.

I will set up daily goals that are ambitious but realistic to make sure they are doing everything in their power to get a job and prevent the consequences from being enacted. I have seen people apply to twenty jobs per day, so I try to use a high benchmark just to give my clients an idea of what is really possible.

Let's say it is mid-August and the parents have put an ultimatum down for starting school in the fall. That leaves almost no time to get registered for classes. Making a plan that gets the client registered within a day or two is the only real option here. If a client is waiting until two weeks before school starts to get registered for classes, then preparing them for the reality of not many classes being open is important.

Regardless of what the contract says, get to work right away in the planning stage for the client because they do need the help and we want to make sure we give our clients every opportunity to succeed. The contract is not a plan to fail, it is a plan to succeed!

While much of the logistical legwork is out of the way, the most difficult phase in the process is the actual follow-through of the plan that we have in place. Ask any football coach. You can draw up the greatest play in the world, but if the players do not run the play correctly, then it is completely worthless. That's the way I view the contract with a failure-to-launch child and their family. We have a great plan in place, but it is up to us to coach the family/client to run the play correctly and up the family/client to actually execute it correctly.

Chapter Fifteen

Clearing the Tower

If the previous chapter uses the metaphor of the launch pad to illustrate where the family/client are in the process, then this phase of treatment definitely is liftoff. At this point, we have done everything that we can do to ensure that the client/family has everything they need for a successful mission. Every plan has been uploaded, the crew has been properly trained, and all systems are a go for launch.

Once the family walks out of my office with the contract in hand, we really get to see how serious our clients are about changing. The one thing that we have to remember is that dysfunction always serves some purpose in a family system. By restructuring the family dynamics and the power structure, those dysfunctions can start to surface. These dysfunctions will be the main reason the plan will blow up shortly after liftoff.

Since this phase of treatment has been more about the parental boundaries and expectations being the drivers of change, it is their issues that will lead to a failure of the mission. Most clients have had years of experience with their parents, and many have seen their parents cave time and time again when they were forced to hold a line with their children. Given this experience, many of our clients do not feel as though this time will be any different and will challenge their parents quickly.

In many cases, when the parents are challenged early in the process, their old dynamics will emerge, and they want to go back to old ways of dealing with things (i.e., yelling, retreating, enabling, etc.). We have to anticipate this happening, and the best way to prevent this from happening is to coach the parents throughout this process. While some parents can be trusted to enforce the contract and you may not have to talk to them for another month, many parents are going to need coaching and accountability along the way.

There is no hard or fast rule on how to identify which parents will need coaching along the way. Typically families where there are high levels of enabling, history of poor boundaries, or a history of poor follow-through are families that I identify as needing additional coaching. Furthermore, in families where the client is refusing to be part of the process, the only way to work with the family system is through the parental system.

It is a good idea to meet with the parents within two weeks of enacting the contract to see how things have been progressing. Very quickly you will see how the child is reacting to the new boundaries, and you will also see if the parents have been able to hold up their end of the bargain as well.

The purpose of the follow-up meetings is to assess several items. First, we want to assess how well the plan is working. The reason why we developed such a specific contract is so that we can concretely measure whether or not a child is making progress. When I ask parents whether or not a child is making progress, we can easily look at specific behaviors to determine whether or not they are.

If the child is not making any progress, it is imperative that we begin to research why there is not any progress being accomplished. Since I am meeting with the parents at this point, I will ask them what they are doing and how they are responding to the lack of progress. There are many pitfalls that parents fall into during the early stages of treatment.

The first pitfall is that they see that there is no progress and they fall back onto their old patterns of behavior. When parents see that their child is not making progress, they cannot overcome their anxiety/fear of their child failing and will try to "help" the child to succeed (i.e., micro-managing, hovering, doing things for them, etc.). Other parents will feel the anger of being taken advantage of and will take their frustration out on the child by yelling at them and threatening them.

Regardless of their reactions, we must address these patterns of behavior with the parents and coach them on how to be effective in this situation. Many parents will not realize that they are falling back into their old patterns again, and simple redirection will help bring them back in line. Many parents feel as though the plan is not working and believe that "their way" is the only way to get them back in line. I try not to tell the parents outright that they are wrong, but I do try to say that the consequences are what are going to police this plan. They have tried "their way" in the past and it has not worked at all, and I tell them why it does not work. If you have a good rapport with the family, you can usually overcome any of these pitfalls and get everybody back with the plan again.

It is important to remember though that many of these family systems are incredibly dysfunctional, and sometimes it is almost impossible to overcome the dysfunction. If we are being honest, many of the parents that we are working with have equally as severe, if not worse, psychological problems than their children. For example, I was recently working with a family and developing a behavioral contract for their son. The son had recurring problems with marijuana abuse, legal problems, emotional stability, no motivation, and all-around poor relationships with the family members. The client was complacent about going into any agreement with the parents because he said that they never stuck to their word and that his mother was "crazier than he was."

After negotiating a contract and getting everything in place, it appeared that we were set and everything was going smoothly . . . for all of four days. One of the clauses in the contract was to just let their son be when he did not want to do something with the family. Instead of this happening, the mother blew up at the son and told him to f-off and that she hated him. She went to church with her family and interpreted the sermon that she was to kick her son out of the house now and even falsely said that everyone in the family told her to kick him out now. So she went home and kicked him out of the house, and the son proceeded to go on a drug bender. Of course she called me back two days later saying that we needed to get him help and do an intervention to get him drug treatment.

Now, I was never able to formally assess the mother, but from what I was able to gather, the mother was getting DBT treatment for borderline personality disorder and this was par for the course with her. When dealing with a parental unit with this level of dysfunction, sometimes it is impossible to get them to stick with the plan. The best thing that you can do is be honest with them and do what you can. More often than not, I have bluntly told parents that they are paying me to help coach this plan and they are not following anything that I tell them. I say that if they do not follow the plan that I have laid out, it is impossible for me to help with the situation and maybe we should refer to another clinician. We have an ethical obligation to refer to another clinician if we are not helping out at all.

Another example of parental dysfunction that sabotages the process is when a parent's anxiety is so great that they cannot overcome it and never follow through on the consequences. For example, I was working with a family recently where the child absolutely refused to be part of the process. The mother was scared that her son would run away or commit suicide if she pushed him too far, so she just let him stay home and play video games all day. The child was eighteen and was supposed to go back to military school for his senior year. The child was angry because when they made the decision to send him to military school the previous year, she defied her husband and lied to her son that if he got good grades, he could come home at the holiday break. She said that she did this because she was anxious about him running away or committing suicide, so she told him that to calm him down.

Of course when the holiday break came and he was not allowed to come home, their son was angry and had no confidence or trust in his parents at all.

He came home from school in June and was angry and miserable the entire time. He lashed out at his parents and refused to do anything. The mother was wavering on letting him stay home for the year and go to a local high school, but the father was adamant about him going back to military school. After going over the pros and cons, it was apparent that military school was the best option. The problem was that their son was eighteen years old, and if they wanted him to go to military school, they would have to be very structured and let him know exactly what would happen if he did not go.

After carefully constructing the contract, the mother's anxiety began to rise, and the parents fought fiercely in my office with the father saying that if she gave in to her son, he was going to move out and divorce her. After de-escalating their conflict, I was able to reframe the situation and get the mother to agree that they really had no other option but to be firm with their son. They were supposed to present the contract to their son that evening and follow up with me the next week with how everything went. That session never came, and I found out that the mother caved in to her son and let him go to a local high school.

This is the worst possible outcome for this family because all the parents did was reinforce the child's negative behavior. They reinforced that if he pouts, yells, screams, threatens suicide, and holds the family hostage, then he will get exactly what he wants. What is also important to note about this family is that they have an older son who has completely failed to launch, and the mother also refuses to push her older son out of fear that "he cannot be pushed too far."

As you can see in the two examples, much of the problem of failure to launch is with the parental system as much as with the child itself. You can construct the best plan possible and coach the parents on exactly what to do, and they are still unable to overcome their dysfunction. These pitfalls are profoundly difficult to overcome and the earlier you identify these pitfalls, the more you are able to address/overcome them before the sabotage the entire plan.

The good thing is that severe dysfunction as described above is not very common, and most situations where parents fall back into old patterns of behavior are easily overcome. If a parent is experiencing anxiety about a lack of progress, it is good to do some minor therapy work with the parents. While I am not their counselor, it is important to explore the root of their anxiety and teach them ways to manage their own anxiety. I know these parents love their children, and because of that love they are anxious about their child failing. What I usually do is state to the parents:

> *I know you love your children and that you want them to be successful. The reason that we are here is because you wanted them to be successful, and we developed a good plan to get them there. I know it goes against what you feel,*

but this plan is the best way to get them there. I can tell you with 100 percent certainty that if you go back to doing the same things, then he will fail. With the plan that we have constructed, maybe we have a 50 percent chance of success. Even though it is a 50/50 shot, I will take that over a 100 percent chance of failure any day of the week.

This is usually the best way to get parents back on the same page because it helps them acknowledge that the plan that we have constructed is the best way to get their child to be successful. Regardless of if they are angry or anxious, the best way to proceed is to manage their own emotions and stick with the plan. In some cases, I will refer a parent to a clinician if too many of their own issues are coming up and need help to process and overcome them.

Another pitfall to be cognizant of are parents having too high/low of expectations for measuring success. Part of our job in the process is to help manage the expectations of the parents. For example, I have had several parents that have set their expectations way too low for the client. While in the contract we had specifics as to what they considered "getting a job," the parents will often lower the bar and say that, "Well, he got out of bed and looked at jobs online. He did not apply to any, but it was a step forward." While it might have been a small step forward, it was not what we contracted for, and the child is not meeting the terms in the contract. Parents in these situations just do not want to enforce consequences on their child because it hurts them to do it. It is important to call parents out on their actions and hold them accountable to the contract and the terms within the contract. If parents begin to waver and lower the bar in one area, then they will do it in another area, and before they know it, the contract is useless.

In another example, I had a family who had expectations in the contract to start school in the fall and required twelve credit hours. They did not mention any other requirements in the contract, and when school started in the fall, they were not happy with him just doing twelve credit hours of class and wanted to put grade requirements on him and also getting a part-time job. I had to temper the expectations of the parents because none of that was discussed in the initial contract, and adding all of those things after the fact makes the contract null and void. It makes the child feel as though his parents will never live up to their end of the bargain and his best is never good enough. Remember, manage the parent's expectations, and if they wish to add more requirements to the contract, wait until the first set of terms in the contract have been met before doing anything else.

These are all the typical pitfalls that I have run into with the families that I have worked with. This is by no means an exhaustive list of every problem that you will run into with your families, but they are the major ones. Planning for these problems and addressing them when they show up will help keep the parents in line and will give the plan the best chance for success.

It is also important to discuss the potential pitfalls that can come up with the child during this phase of the process. When flying an airplane, the take-off is when a plane is at its most vulnerable stage. If any type of failure happens during this phase, there are not many things a pilot can do to save the airplane. Just like an airplane, the initial weeks of this new plan are when the client is at its most vulnerable state. If any major issues arise, it will have a greater effect now than at any point in treatment.

With many of our clients, they are being held accountable for their actions for the very first time in their lives. They are being forced to try hard for the first time in their lives, and their resources have never been taxed like this. I liken it to working out for the first time. If a person never works out, then their stamina will be low, and if they push themselves too hard, they will collapse. The same goes for our clients, meaning that their stamina is low and it is imperative that we help coach them on how to work hard and conserve energy at the same time.

Some of the things that you can see from your clients are them trying hard in the first few weeks, but quickly running out of motivation and energy when they are not getting the results that they want or just getting tired of trying. With clients who are going to school, you will see them studying, doing all of their assignments, going to class every day, and even getting good grades. Then, slowly but surely they begin to lose their head of steam and begin slacking off. It starts off as one assignment they do not turn in, cramming for an exam at the last second, skipping one class. It starts off subtly and before they know it, they are behind in their classes and right back into their old patterns of behavior.

It is important to assess for these behaviors and to address them as soon as you see them. I often call my clients out on their behavior and go back to the MI work that we did in the beginning to refocus them and get them back on track. While it is easy to automatically assume that our clients are lazy and that is the reason for the drop-off, we have to realize that many of our clients really do not know how to be successful in school or whatever it is they want to do. The drop-off is often the result of poor coping skills or poor work skills. Just like with working out, there is a right way to work out and a wrong way to work out. It is our job to make sure they are doing things the right way.

This can include coaching them on how to study, when to study, how often, how to take breaks, self-care, and working smarter, not harder. If after all of this coaching the client is still having problems, they may very well have underlying learning disabilities or ADHD. As we discussed in earlier chapters, many of these issues do not present until their systems are taxed, and that usually happens in college. If the client never applied themselves until now, then this is when those issues will arise. If I feel as though a deeper psychological problem is present, I will send them off for a full educational battery to determine if any learning disabilities are present. If so, then we can refer out to a psychiatrist for medications, a specialist for learning disabilities, and even accommodations with the school.

Another pitfall that can come up during this time is outward symptoms of depression and anxiety. Like I said earlier, many of these clients are trying for the first time in their lives, with many of them never having wanted to try because they fear failing. Sometimes it is easier to not try at all than to try and fail. When we begin pushing these clients to go to school, work, and so forth, they are being forced to confront their problems for the very first time. What I see often in my clients is that as soon as they get one bad grade or do not get a job after an interview, the negative thinking returns and they begin to doubt themselves.

As soon as the negative thinking begins, motivation wanes, energy levels go down, pessimistic thinking ensues, and they go back to their old patterns of behaving. It can happen quickly, and once it begins, it can be difficult to get them back on track. With clients who are at risk for these problems, it is important to keep them motivated and thinking positive. Preparing them for possible failure is important because it keeps their expectations grounded and realistic. When failures do happen, it is important to process what happened and make a plan to correct the problems that occurred.

As the client tries harder and realizes that they have no option but to succeed, the added stress can increase their anxiety levels. Many of these clients have little to no stress coping skills, and it is important to teach clients how to manage stress during this phase of treatment. I am an advocate of teaching mindfulness, meditation, and progressive relaxation. I often teach my clients these skills in the beginning of our work so that they have these skills even before stress does occur. I also help stress the importance of finding a good work balance and making sure they make time for self-care activities.

Planning for these problems will help keep your client motivated, mentally healthy, calm, and positive—all which are required for long-term success.

The last major pitfall to be aware of with clients in this phase is boundary testing. Many of these clients for years have been manipulating their parents and seeing what they are able to get away with. Some clients generally do want to progress in life, but some are hell-bent on not changing at all. As soon as the contract gets enacted, you will see some clients pushing the boundaries of what is expected out of them. Maybe it is waking up an hour later than what is required, or maybe it is taking a chance and not applying for jobs on a particular day. Whatever it is they are doing, it is important to call your clients out on their boundary testing and asking them what they really are doing.

When I ask my clients this question, some truly believe that their parents will never hold to their bottom line. If they feel as though their parents will cave in, then they have no reason to do anything that is expected of them because they see no consequence. Some clients will calculate in their mind the chance that their parents will hold to their bottom line and will take a calculated risk if they feel as though the chances are low.

With clients who are testing the boundaries, I try to get them to understand that mom and dad mean business and I do not feel as though they are going to cave. I try to create cognitive dissonance by laying out all of the evidence to suggest that they will hold to their bottom line and how the consequences of inaction will affect them. I try to get them to realize how great of a chance that they are taking and to see if doing nothing is really worth the risk. For many clients, this will help motivate them to make some changes, but for some . . . you cannot get through to them, and ultimately they may have to pay the piper in the end.

Chapter Sixteen

Houston, We Have a Problem

I didn't go in to this business to fail, and I sure as hell didn't write this book to teach clinicians how to fail. But we have to be realistic that we are going to have clients fail. It is just the reality of the situation. Sometimes it will be the parents' fault, sometimes the client's, and many times the result of both. Regardless of whose fault it is, we can be sure that we did everything in our power to try and make this plan work.

So how do we really define failure? I guess in my mind it's very simple . . . the client does not reach their goals. We started on this journey to get a child launched into their future. Whether it is for them to be successful in school, financially independent, clean and sober, and so forth, our goal was to get them there. If the client does not achieve the terms outlined in the contract, then we consider the plan a failure . . . right . . . or is it a failure?

When we are talking about a client, our ultimate goal is to get them to where they need to be. Of course we would like to get them there as fast as humanly possible, but sometimes we have to settle for getting there period. In my experience, I believe that sometimes we have to analyze the short-term goals of a client versus the long-term goals. Many parents will want to look at the short-term goals of getting them independent, but often there are too many obstacles to accomplish that. So we do the next best thing, we use failure as a means to create success.

As I spoke about in the beginning of the book, when we don't allow a child to fail, they never learn the consequences of their actions and never learn how to handle failure. That is a huge reason why the child is in the current situation to begin with. So it is really no surprise when a child does not meet the terms of the contract because they simply to do not believe there will be any consequences to failing. Furthermore, the child has never experienced any hardship or felt any consequences for their poor choices in life.

Without those experiences, what is to stop them from continuing to make bad choices?

If we do not pay our cell phone bill, the phone will get turned off and our credit will take a hit. As a result, we make sure that we never put ourselves in that situation again. We work extra hours, cut out unnecessary expenditures, and so forth. We do whatever is necessary to avoid that negative consequence again.

With our clients, they have never experienced any consequences, so they do not have experiences like that to draw from. Without those experiences, the client feels no pressure at all to avoid anything. So, we have to create those experiences for them . . . which is exactly what failing will do.

When a client fails to live up to the expectations in the contract, the parents have to exercise the consequences in the contract without fail or hesitation. If the consequence is for the child to be kicked out of the house, then the parents have to kick them out of the house. If they have to cut the child off financially, then they cut the child off right away. It does not matter what the consequence is or how severe it is, if the parent does not exercise the consequence, then they are actually hurting their child.

This is a difficult concept for some parents to understand—that punishing their child and making them uncomfortable is a good thing. It goes against many parents' instincts, which is to do no harm to their child. But the truth is that sometimes you have to punish a child for them to learn a lesson. It is only through hardship that people can learn certain life lessons.

For example, I had a client whose family had set an ultimatum that if he did not have a job by a certain date, he was going to be kicked out of the house on that date and would be 100 percent financially independent. The client did not feel as though his parents would follow through on the consequence and took the risk of doing nothing and seeing what would happen. When the date was approaching and the parents saw no progress from him, I received a call from the mother crying that she did not want to kick the child out of the house. She stated to me, "What is he going to do? Where will he live?"

I calmly said to her that it was not her responsibility to worry about that. I said that if somebody does not work and earn money in this world, then they will be homeless. Your son has to realize that you are not going to support him for the rest of his life, and you let him know what was going to happen if he did not get a job. By following through on the consequence and kicking him out, he will know what it feels like to not have money and not know where he is going to live. It will give him the emotions and thoughts necessary to realize that he does not like this feeling and will do anything in his power to not get back there again.

When the date came and her son did not have a job, she kicked him out of the house and he slept on friends' couches for two weeks. After a few days, his friends would get sick of him leeching off of them, and he would be asked to leave. After doing this for about a month, the client could not stand it anymore and finally got a job at a local sandwich shop. When he got his job, he was allowed to move back in and a new contract was established.

By allowing the child to fail, we turned it into an experience that eventually led him to success. When we make the contracts, sometimes I know that the client will not meet the expectations. It does not bother me, because if they meet the goals of the contract, that is awesome. But if they fail and the parents hold their ground, I know that is what is best for the child, and as a result, they will eventually succeed as a result of the failure

While I would like to pretend that every failure can be reframed as a positive, I really cannot say that all failures are an eventual success. There are certain populations of children who, no matter what, we or the families cannot get through to them and get them to change their behavior and progress through life.

When we are dealing with a client with substance abuse issues, there is the very sad reality that not all addicts are going to get better. These are the most difficult failure-to-launch clients because there is the fact that if the client does not get better, then they could go to jail, kill somebody else, or kill themselves. Parents know this, and those facts are why parents will continue to enable their child.

If a client in this situation does not live up to their end of the contract, then a parent has no option but to enforce the consequences and hold to their bottom line. I always tell parents that there should always be a treatment option for substance abusers if they were to relapse. If a client in this situation relapses or continues to use, then they should always have the option for treatment. If they successfully complete a treatment program, then a new contract can be negotiated. However, if they relapse/continue to use and they refuse treatment, then the parents must cut ties with their child and allow them to feel the consequences of their actions.

The only control that a parent has on this situation is to not contribute to their substance abuse issues. I always tell parents, "If you continue to support your child and enable their use, I can say with 100 percent certainty that your child is going to go to jail, kill somebody, or kill themselves. If you hold to your bottom line and kick them out and cut off support, then maybe there is a 50 percent chance those things are going to happen, I will take a 50 percent chance of success over a 100 percent chance of failure."

For many parents, the thought of taking a drastic option such as kicking them out of the house and not having any contact is too much for them to manage on their own. In cases such as this, it may be necessary to bring in a professional interventionist who can mediate the intervention and coach the parents on how to hold their bottom lines. Even if the client chooses to go in for treatment, it is imperative that the parents hold to all of their bottom lines and make sure the client is continuing with their treatment. Many parents have held their bottom lines and sent the child off to treatment, but allowed them back in to house after quitting treatment and starting the process back over again.

If the child chooses to not go to treatment and decided to leave the house, it is necessary to continue to work with the family to help them deal with their own anxiety about kicking their child out of the house. Furthermore, you can continue to help guide them on holding to their bottom line and not letting the child manipulate them and let them back in to their lives without getting help. It is important to note that treatment is always on the table. If a child refuses treatment initially but later decides that they need help, that offer is always on the table.

The other populations that you can expect to have a low rate of success will be with severe mental health problems. When we have clients who have been diagnosed with schizophrenia, schizoaffective, and autism spectrum, we cannot be entirely sure that they will be able to function independently. One of the biggest concerns that I hear from parents of children with these disorders is whether they will have to take care of their child for the rest of their life.

I wish I could say that they will be able to, but in reality it is difficult to know what a person is able to accomplish. That is why in these cases, we make a contract, so that we can really determine what they are able to accomplish. If they are able to become more independent, that is great. However, as time goes on, it will become apparent if they are able to or not. If the client is truly unable to function on their own (i.e., hold down a job, go to school, live on their own, and so forth), then parents have a very difficult question to ask themselves. That question is whether or not they have the patience to take care of their adult child.

Many parents do not have the patience to do that, and there is nothing wrong with that. If that is the answer they give, then having the child live in a group home and/or going on disability is a realistic option. For adults with severe mental health disabilities, there are several great resources available to them. This way they can be out of the house and in an environment where they can live somewhat independently but with supervision.

If a parent decides that they do have the patience and resources to support their child, it is important to make a contract that includes achievable items such as taking medication, seeing a counselor, no aggressive behavior, and so forth.

It is not easy for a parent to acknowledge that an adult child will never achieve the dreams that they dreamt for them. It is the saddest part of our jobs when we have to level with parents that their child has limited upward mobility in life. There are several support groups for the parents who are in these situations, and I always recommend continued counseling to help them comes to terms with these facts.

Chapter Seventeen

Houston, We Have Liftoff

I think one of the most fulfilling things about our jobs is when we have the chance to not only help people, but literally change the trajectory of their lives. That is why I love working with this population because when we succeed in helping these clients, the evidence is readily apparent, and you can see where their lives will forever be changed.

As our clients progress through their goals, it is important to continue to coach them and point out all of the success that they are making. I will often point out what their life was like when they first came into my office and where they are going now. While the progress might be readily apparent to us, sometimes clients have a difficult time seeing the progress that they are making. I have had several clients who said, "Yeah, I have great grades at community college, but I want to be graduated by now."

It is important to remember that many of our clients will be in their early twenties, and if they would have tried this hard in the beginning, they would be either graduating or close to graduating. Even though they are making progress, a part of them believes they are still behind and any progress can be tarnished. So it is important to manage expectations and keep them on the right path.

Another important item to note is to make sure that you help coach the parents on how to give feedback about progress as well. The family system has been in such a negative feedback loop for so long and it is difficult to break that cycle. When the child is making progress, some parents will fall into "Well, why should I pat him on the back when they are doing what they should be doing?" What I tell parents is that as your child is making progress, give them positive feedback about the progress that they are making. This helps create good will between the parent and the child and also helps keep the child motivated because other people are seeing that they are doing good.

In a perfect scenario, we didn't even have to get the parents involved, and the plan that we developed was purely maintained by the client and the clinician. In these cases, the client has a long-term plan and will not need any additional planning or goal setting. In cases where a contract had to be enacted by the parents, additional contracting may be necessary once terms have been met in the original contract.

What I instruct parents to do is once the original terms have been met, determine what the next steps in the process are and insert those goals into the original contract. As their child moves further along, it is important that the parents have expectations and consequences in the contract, although the consequences can begin to soften as the child moves further along.

While I think we need to celebrate a child's progress and provide positive feedback for their accolades, we have to remember that the only reason many children make it this far is because of the boundaries that we put in place. If parents remove all of the boundaries too quickly, then the child will likely fall back into their old ways. I liken this idea to having braces. If you take the braces off too soon, the teeth will go back to where they were. So once the teeth are where they need to be, the braces are kept on there for an extended period of time until the doctor knows that the new teeth positions are solidified. Even once the braces are removed, a less restrictive retainer is used to make sure the teeth stay in place. You do not want to throw out all the progress of two years of braces. The same goes for our boundaries, you do not want to throw out a year of progress.

So how do we know when a child has fully launched? Well . . . there really is no simple answer that I can give you. What I have found in my experience is that the goals we initially set in the beginning are not the final goals toward the end. In the beginning, many parents have set basic goals for their child such as just getting a job and going to school. But as those goals get met, then higher-order goals begin to get set, such as moving out, becoming financially independent, going to a four-year college, graduate school, and so forth.

I think parents and our clients can make a huge mistake if they meet the initial goals and stop there. Of course in the beginning we are looking at simple goals, but I always think my clients are capable of more. I often tell my clients that I am greedy and I am going to want more out of them. So as clients are approaching the end of the initial goals, work with the clients and their families on what the next step is and how to maintain expectations so they can achieve the next level of goals.

The main goal of failure to launch is to get adult children launched into their future, with a huge part of that being independent self-sufficient adults. It is important to work with families on slowly but surely transferring self-responsibility to the child.

An adult will be able to fully support themselves, which means that they are making money and able to pay their own bills. While in the beginning it will be difficult for a child working a part-time job to afford to cover all of their bills, it is imperative that parents slowly start to transfer individual responsibilities over to them.

In the later contracts, parents should slowly transfer over responsibilities such as car insurance, cell phone bill, utilities, and so forth over to the client. If you transfer all of them over at once, that may be too much for them, so it is wise for parents to do this slowly. I liken it to slowly putting weight on a healing broken leg. If you put too much weight on it too soon, the leg will get re-injured. So to prevent that, we slowly rehab the leg and slowly put weight back on it. Eventually it will be strong enough to support all the weight. That is the exact approach that I tell parents to apply to future contracts and expectations.

Slowly but surely, parents will see their child maturing in front of them and watch them become launched self-sufficient adults. It is interesting when I write adults because for most of this book I was discussing their children as if they were young children. The very nature of their relationship almost infantilized the child in a way.

When their child becomes an adult in every sense of the word, the relationship between the parents and the child has to mature as well. For many parents, this may be their first child and have never experienced what it is like to have an adult relationship with their child. What does that even look like anyway?

The example I like to give is from my own life. Last year, my wife and I decided to go a concert at the Gorge Amphitheatre in George, Washington, for Labor Day weekend. It was a three-day concert, and we rented an RV with a group of friends. When I told my mother what we were doing, she said that she couldn't believe that we would fly halfway across the country for a concert and then spend all that money on an RV.

Now, did my mom express her disagreement with our decision . . . sure. Did she say that I could not go? . . . Nope. She couldn't because I am an adult and that is not her job to tell me what to do anymore. Since I am an adult and I make my own money, she does not have any power over how I spend my money. I do love my mom and very much take into consideration her opinion, but since we have an adult relationship, there are certain boundaries that cannot be crossed.

This is my reference point for how an adult relationship should be structured. Every family is different, and I respect the fact that not everybody is going to agree with my view 100 percent. But we have to help parents understand that one of the biggest contributors to the failure-to-launch problem is an enmeshed and enabling family system. We have to help create better boundaries to ensure that the same problems do not return in the future.

This is a good problem to have, and most families adjust to it with no problems at all. One of the questions that parents ask me toward the end of this process is what their financial role should be in their child's life. This is an important question to discuss because the vast majority of these failure-to-launch clients will be from affluent families. What is an affluent family sharing their good fortune with their children, and what is contributing to failure to launch?

When I was going through undergraduate and graduate school, my parents helped me out a lot along the way. It was really nice having parents who were able to help out when I was short on rent some months or when my bank account was running low and I wanted to go out with my friends.

I believe that there is nothing wrong with an affluent family sharing their good fortune with their children. Heck, I know that if I am able to, I will do the same for my children. It really helped me out in my life, and I think it can do a lot of good. I think it becomes an issue when the child looks at the money as a birthright or an entitlement. If the child feels as though they are entitled to having financial support and do not appreciate the money, that is when it becomes a problem.

This is a delicate balance for our newly launched children because they are finally becoming independent and supporting themselves, and we do not want to disrupt the progress that has been made. I think it is difficult for me to draw an exact line in the sand and say this is when you give money and this is when you don't. The best way to handle this is to just discuss with the parents this very topic and make them aware of what is enabling and what is helping. If they feel as though their child is expecting help and using their money as an excuse to not take their own responsibility, then they should draw back any support.

At this point, everything is pretty much out of your hands as a clinician. You have taught the family everything that they need to know and have developed a plan with every contingency accounted for. The client's know what they have to do and have every psychological tool necessary to get there.

The thing to remember here is that our job is to provide insight to our clients that they would not be able to see on their own. Based on that insight, we develop interventions based on our education and years of experience. While it would be more lucrative, I do not believe in making my client and their families dependent on me for help. I believe that we give them everything they need to generate success and growth on their own and be able to learn from past mistakes to overcome future mistakes.

I wrote this book so that I could pass on everything that I have learned from my practice so that you can incorporate it in to your practice. I hope everything in this book will be helpful to you, and I know that if you apply what I have discussed in this book, you will help launch your clients into their future.

Afterword

When I share my story with people, I have been met with surprise at how far I have come. I guess to other people it might look like it is not characteristic to my current neurotic self, but for me . . . it is still a daily chore to stay motivated and stay on top of things. I still loathe getting up before 9:00 a.m., and I always procrastinate on everything that I do (cough—this book—cough).

It is important for me to express this truth to you because it is vital to understand that for many of your failure-to-launch clients, they will struggle with motivation and a consistent work ethic for the rest of their lives.

I know myself very well, and I know that if I begin to let my foot off the throttle, then I know that I have the potential to be right back where I began. I know that I have to be honest with myself and make sure that I continue to do the things that have kept me in line. When I tell myself that I can do my case notes tomorrow, I know it is BS, so at that very moment I get my notes out and get caught up. When I tell myself that I can write some chapters tomorrow, I get my laptop out and I start writing. When my wife asks me to get the coffee maker ready for the morning, and I say that I will do it before I go to bed, I know I will forget if I wait, so I get up at that moment and do it then.

I do not know why I have such a difficulty with doing the things that most people do with little or no effort. Maybe it's ADHD or just being lazy, but I do know what habits work, and I keep doing them because it keeps me honest.

I encourage you to keep this admission in the back of your minds because while it might be more lucrative to have your clients come back every year or so when they relapse, I always tell my clients that I hope I do not see them again, because I want the problem solved the first time I see them.

References

Amen, D. (2001). *Healing ADD.* New York: Berkley Publishing Group.
American Psychiatric Association, Eds. (2000). *Diagnostical and statistical manual of mental disorders.* Washington, DC: American Psychological Association.
Arnett, J. (2004). *Emerging adulthood: The winding road from adolescence to early adulthood.* New York: Oxford University Press.
Bakalar, J. B., & Grinspoon L. (1990 May). The harmfulness tax: A new approach to drug control. *Hosp Community Psychiatry 41*(5): 483.
Baron-Cohen, S. (1995). *Mindblindness: An essay on autism and theory of mind.* Cambridge: MIT Press/Bradford Books.
Baumeister, Roy F., Campbell, Jennifer D., Krueger, Joachim I., & Vohs, Kathleen D. (2005). Exploding the self-esteem myth. *Scientific American.*
Bugen, L. (2010). *Stuck on me: Missing you.* Missouri: ACFEI Media.
Bushman, B., & Anderson, C. (2001). Violent video games and hostile expectations. *Journal of Personality and Social Psychology 28*(12).
Carter, B., & McGoldrick, M. (1999). *The expanded family life cycle.* Massachusetts: Allyn & Bacon.
Fields, R. D. (2005). Myelination: An overlooked mechanism of synaptic plasticity? *Neuroscientist 11*(6).
Gomes, J., Song, T., Godwin, L., & Toriello, P. (2011). Prescription stimulant abuse on university campuses. *Journal of Human Behavior in the Social Environment 21*(7).
Hergenhahn, B. R. (2005). *An introduction to the history of psychology.* California: Wadsworth.
Isaacson, E., Ed. (1991). *Chemical dependency: Theoretical approaches and strategies working with individuals and families.* New York: Haworth Press.
Johnson, Sharon L. (2003). *Therapist's guide to substance abuse intervention.* New York: Academic Press.
Kahn, M. (2002). *Basic Freud: Psychoanalytic thought for the twenty-first century.* New York: Basic Books.
Kalat, James W. (2001). *Biological psychology* (7th ed.). Canada: Wadsworth.
Kanner, L. (1948). Irrelevant and metaphorical language in early infantile autism. *American Journal of Psychiatry 103*(2): 161–164.
Lupton, R. A., Chapman, K. J., & Weiss, J. E. (2000). A cross-national exploration of business students' attitudes, perceptions, and tendencies toward academic dishonesty. *Journal of Education for Business 75*(4).

Meier, M. H. et al. (2012). Persistent cannabis users show neuropsychological decline from childhood to midlife. *Proceedings of the National Academy of Sciences of the United States of America.*

Miller, W., & Rollick, S. (1991). *Motivation interviewing: Preparing people for change.* New York: Guilford Press.

Minuchin, S. (1972). *Families & family therapy.* Cambridge: Harvard University Press.

Rogers, C. (1951). *Client-centered therapy: Its current practice, implications and theory.* Boston: Houghton.

Rotgers, F., Morgensterm, J., & Walters, S. (2003). *Treating substance abuse.* New York: Guilford Press.

Twenge, J. (2006). *Generation me.* New York: Simon & Schuster.

Twenge, J., & Campbell, W. (2009). *The narcissism epidemic.* New York: Simon & Schuster.

Wilson, W., Matthew, R., Turkington, T., Hawk, T., Coleman, R. E., & Provenzale, J. (2000). Brain morphological changes and early marijuana use: a magnetic resonance and positron emission tomography study. *Journal of Addictive Diseases* 19(1): 1–22.

Index

ACG. *See* anterior cingulate gyrus
achievement, high level, 91
ADD. *See* attention deficit disorder
addiction, 20; comorbidity with, 27; enabling, 31. *See also* substance abuse
addiction brain types, 69–72; anxiety-driven, 71; compulsive, 70; impulsive, 70–71; impulsive-compulsive, 71; panic disorder temporal lobe, 72; sad, 71
ADHD. *See* attention deficit hyperactivity disorder
adolescents: ADD of, 54; depression signs for, 45; egocentrism of, 25
adult: ADD of, 54; demographic shift in maturity of, 11–12; relationships of, 159
adulthood, emerging, 12; age of possibilities during, 13; identity exploration during, 13; instability during, 13; self-focused age of life, 13; transition feeling during, 13
adult maturity, demographic shift in, 11; birth control rise in 60s/70s, 12; college attendance increase, 12
age of possibilities during emerging adulthood, 13
Amen, Daniel, 55
amphetamine, 74–76; ADHD medication, 74; chronic effects of abuse of, 75–76; cocaine, 75; dopamine and, 74, 76; methamphetamine, 74–75; prescription, abuse of, 74; SPECT on, 75
anterior cingulate gyrus (ACG), 46; compulsive addiction brain type, 70; impulsive-compulsive addiction brain type and, 71; overfocused anxiety/depression and, 46
anti-depressant, SSRI: for PDD, 67; temporal lobe anxiety/depression aggravation by, 45
anxiety, 32, 41–49, 149; brain vulnerability and, 42; during career and life coaching, 103; depression coexistence with, 44; GABA for, 48; life stress and, 42; of loving parent enabler, 36–37; opiate abuse and, 77; pure anxiety, 43–44; social, 7, 105, 108
anxiety/depression: overfocused, 46–47; temporal lobe, 45–46
anxiety-driven addiction brain type, 71
Arnett, Jeffrey, 12
arrogance of millennials, 19
Asperger, Hans, 64
Asperger's syndrome, 7, 62, 118; DSM-IV criteria for, 61–62; early intervention for, 63
assessment: ADHD, LD, 5; behavior, 148; vocational, 6, 93–99
attention deficit disorder (ADD), 51; of adolescents, 54; adults, substance abuse and, 44, 52; of adults, 54; causes of, 54;

167

of children, 53; classic, 55–56; inattentive, 55; limbic, 55, 57; overfocused, 55–56; prison population with, 52; ring of fire, 55, 57; temporal lobe, 55–57; throughout lifespan, 53–54
attention deficit disorder treatment, 57–58; holistic, 57, 59; ineffective, 58–59; issues, 58; lifestyle changes, 58; supplement strategies, 58
attention deficit hyperactivity disorder (ADHD), 51–59, 106, 148; amphetamine medication for, 74; assessment, 5; causes of, 54; of children, 53; cyclic mood disorders and, 47; DSM-IV on types of, 55; myths, 51–52; PFC, BG, DLS and, 51; signs and symptoms of, 52–53; types of, 55–57; undiagnosed, 7
attention deficit hyperactivity disorder symptoms: disorganization, 53; distractibility, 53; follow through, poor, 53; internal supervision, poor, 53
autism: early intervention for, 63; fMRI for, 65; gene abnormality causes, 64–65; genetic factors for, 64; infantile, 63–64; MR and, 64; MRI for, 65; PET Scan for, 65; post-mortem studies, 65; prevalence of, 64; SPECT Scan for, 65
autonomy, in MI, 85
avoidance: as enabling behavior, 35; of millennials, 21

baby boomers, 19–20; counter-culture movement of, 19; drug use of, 20; living the dream, 13; peace and, 19
bailing out of trouble enabling behavior, 34–35
basal ganglia (BG): ADHD and, 51; anxiety-driven addiction brain type and, 71; cyclic mood disorders and, 47; depression and, 37; DLS and, 44; overfocused anxiety/depression and, 46; pure anxiety and, 43
basic interest scales in SII, 97
Baumeister, Roy F., 14
behavior assessment, 148
BG. *See* basal ganglia
bipolar disorder, 42, 47
birth control increase in 60s/70s, 12

Bleuler, Eugen, 63
borderline personality disorder, 32, 145
boundary: setting by parent, 117–118, 158; testing, 149–150
brain: ACG of, 46, 70, 71; BG of, 37, 43, 44, 46–47, 51, 71; cocaine and, 75; DLS of, 44, 46–47, 51, 71; dopamine in, 48, 74, 76; encephalization process within, 43; frontal lobe, 43, 46; limbic system, 58; marijuana and, 72; PFC, 51, 58, 70–71; serotonin, 48; TL of, 45; vulnerability, anxiety and, 42
Briggs, Katharine, 95
Bugen, Larry, 17

Campbell, David, 96
Campbell, Jennifer D., 14
career and life coaching, 101–109; anxiety during, 103; career path worksheet, 104–106; counseling compared to, 102–103; fear and, 103; homework and, 101; indecision and, 103; job interview skills, 108; liability from, 102; short-term goals and, 106–108
career choice, 91–99; clinical interview questions for, 94–95; high level achievement and, 91; lack of direction for, 92–93; vocational assessment for, 6, 93–99
career path worksheet, 104–106
Center for Medicinal Cannabis Research, 73
character development, 130
cheating by students, 15
children: ADD, ADHD of, 53; depression signs for, 45; feeling sorry for, parents' game of, 37; overindulgence of, 26; parents' low influence on, 18
choice: career, 91–99; motivation to change as, 82–83
classic ADD, 55–56
client categories: directionless, 5–6; enabling family systems, 7–8; lazy, entitled, unmotivated, 4–5; undiagnosed mental health disorders, 6–7
clinical interview, 93–95; questions for career choice, 94–95; questions in, 93–95; school grade question in, 95

coaching: career and life, 101–109; of client, 148–150; of parents, 143–147, 157
cocaine, 75
cognitive behavioral techniques for PDD, 67
cognitive effects of marijuana, 72–73
cognitive flexibility, ACG for, 46
collaboration, in MI, 85
college and education: attendance increase in, 12; contract and, 124–125; contract expectations, of parents, 130
comorbidity with addiction, 27
compulsive addiction brain type, 70
confidentiality, 81–82, 112–113
consequences, in contract, 123, 152, 158
contract, 121–133; college, 124–125; consequences in, 123, 152, 158; economics consideration in, 123, 129–130; expectations, of parents, 129–130; expectations specificity in, 122–123; on financial support, 125; informal expectations and, 121; language of, 124; measurable goals in, 133; mental illness and, 126–128; negotiation phase, 122; parent's role in, 132; penalties, 123, 130–131, 158; revision of, 159; sample, 128–131, 132; substance abuse and, 126
contract presentation to client, 135–141; contract session, 140–141; family session, 136–140; parents on client lack of progress, 136; signed agreement during, 141
core mindfulness, 140
counseling: coaching compared to, 102–103; theory, 9
counter-culture movement of baby boomers, 19
crisis management in family session, 139
cyclic mood disorders, 47–48; ADHD and, 47; BG, DLS and, 47; bipolar disorder, 42, 47; cyclothymia, 47; panic attacks, 47; PMDD, 47; symptoms of, 47–48
cyclothymia, 47

deep limbic system (DLS): ADHD and, 51; cyclic mood disorders and, 47; depression and, 44; overfocused anxiety/depression and, 46; sad addiction brain type and, 71
defensive reaction, 29
delayed gratification, 26
depression, 26–27, 32, 149; anxiety coexistence with, 44; BG and, 37; brain vulnerability and, 42; DLS and, 44; life stress and, 42; opiate abuse and, 77; pure depression, 44; signs for, 45. See also anxiety/depression
depressive disorder, 42
Diagnostic and Statistical Manual for Mental Illness IV (DSM-IV): on ADHD types, 55; Asperger's Syndrome criteria, 61–62; on narcissistic personality disorder criteria, 24–25; PDD classification by, 61
dichotomies, of MBTI, 95–96
directionless client, 5–6
discrepancy development principle, of MI, 89
disorganization, as ADHD symptom, 53
distractibility, as ADHD symptom, 53
DL phenylalanine supplement, 58
DMS-IV. See Diagnostic and Statistical Manual for Mental Illness IV
dopamine: amphetamines and, 74, 76; 5-HTP for increased levels of, 48
drug abuse. See substance abuse
DSL. See deep limbic system
dysfunction, family systems role of, 38, 143–146
dysthymia, 44
dysthymic disorder, 42

early intervention, for Asperger's syndrome and autism, 63
eating disorders, 46
education. See college and education
ego, 26
egocentrism, 25, 136; neurological development and, 25
Ellis, Albert, 87
emerging adulthood. See adulthood, emerging
emotion management, 137
empathy expression principle, of MI, 86
enabler, loving parent, 36–38, 111, 117, 159; anxiety of, 36–37; feeling sorry for

their children game, 37; hidden potential game, 37–38
enabling behaviors, 31–38; avoidance, 35; bailing out of trouble, 34–35; common, 33–34; giving another chance, 35; operant conditioning and, 34; reasons for, 36
enabling family system client, 7–8
encephalization within brain, 43
entitlement, 16, 26; childhood overindulgence and, 26; of millennials, 21. *See also* lazy, entitled, unmotivated client
evocation, in MI, 85
expectations, of parents: in contract, 128–130; informal, 121; on measuring success, 147; specificity of, 122–123
expectations management, of client, 157
external pressure, as motivation to change, 81

failure in working plan, 151–154; allowing client to fail, 152–153; contract consequences and, 152; short-term goals, 151
family empowerment, 111–118; client-patient confidentiality and, 112–113; mental illness and, 116; parent boundary setting, 117–118, 158; parent questions for, 114; parents' goals and, 114–115; power analysis in, 116; spousal dysfunction and, 113; substance abuse issues and, 116
family session before launch, 136–140; blamer client in, 138; core mindfulness and, 140; crisis management in, 139; denier client in, 138; emotion management during, 137; follow-through and, 141; redirecting in, 137; refereeing of, 137; setting daily goals, 141; shutdown of client in, 138; summarization in, 139–140
family systems theory, 9; dysfunction role in, 38, 143–146
fear, career and life coaching and, 103
feedback: on MBTI, 96; on SII, 97–98
feeling sorry for their children game, 37
financial support, 125, 160
5-HTP, for dopamine level increase, 48

fMRI for autism, 65
follow through, poor, as ADHD symptom, 53
follow up session with parents, 144
Freud, Sigmund, 26, 29
frontal lobe, 43, 46

GABA (gamma aminobutyric acid): for anxiety, 48; for TL, 58
gamma aminobutyric acid. *See* GABA
gene abnormality causes of autism, 64–65
Generation Me and The Narcissism Epidemic (Twinge), 15
genetic factors for autism, 64
giving another chance enabling behavior, 35
goals: for family empowerment, 114–115; measurable, in contract, 133; setting daily, 141; short-term, 106–108, 151
grandiose type of narcissism, 17

head trauma of TL and frontal lobe, 46
Healing ADHD: The Six Different Types of ADHD (Amen), 55
health insurance, MI use of, 84
heroin, 77
hidden potential game, 37–38
holistic treatment, for ADD, 57, 59
Holland, John, 96
Holland codes, in vocational assessment, 96–97
homework, 101
human experience, pain of, 21
humanistic psychology, 14

ICD-10 classification for PDD, 61
identity exploration, 26; during emerging adulthood, 13
impulse control, 34
impulsive addiction brain type, 70–71; characteristics of, 71; PFC and, 70–71
impulsive-compulsive addiction brain type: ACG and, 71; PFC and, 71
inattentive ADD, 55–56
indecision, career and life coaching and, 103
ineffective ADD treatment, 58–59
infantile autism, 63–64
infants, depression signs for, 45

Index 171

instability, during emerging adulthood, 13
intelligence quotient (IQ), marijuana and, 73
internal supervision, poor, as ADHD symptom, 53
Internet, 18
in-vivo exposure therapy, 108
IQ. *See* intelligence quotient

job interview skills, 108
Johnson, Samuel, 22
Jung, Carl, 95

Kanner, Leo, 63
Krueger, Joachim I., 14

language of contract, 124
lazy, entitled, unmotivated client, 4–5; ADHD, LD and, 5; behavioral/psychological problem with, 5
learning disability (LD), 106, 148; assessment, 5; prison population with, 52
liability, from career and life coaching, 102
lifestyle changes for ADD, 58
limbic ADD, 57
limbic system, DL phenylalanine supplement for, 58
living the dream, baby boomers on, 13
L-tyrosine supplement, for PFC, 58

management: crisis, in family session, 139; emotion, 137; expectations, of client, 157; medication, 45, 48–49, 67; pain, by opiates, 76
marijuana, 72–74; brain and, 72; cognitive effects of, 72–73; IQ and, 73; medicinal use of, 73; SPECT on effect of, 73
Maslow, Abraham, 14
MBTI. *See* Myers-Briggs Type Indicator
medical profession, MI use of, 84
medication management, 48–49; antidepressant, SSRI, 45, 67; mood stabilizers, for PDD, 67. *See also* supplements
medicinal use of marijuana, 73
Meier, Madeline, 73
mental health disorders client, 6–7, 154

mental illness: ADD, 51–59; ADHD, 5, 7, 47, 51–59, 74, 106, 148; anxiety, 7, 32, 36–37, 41–49, 77, 103, 105, 108, 149; anxiety/depression, 45–47; Asperger's syndrome, 7, 61–63, 118; autism, 63–66; borderline personality disorder, 32, 145; contracts for, 126, 127–128; cyclic mood disorders, 47–48; depression, 26–27, 32, 37, 42–44, 77, 149; family empowerment and, 116; LD, 5, 52, 106, 148; mood disorders, 41–49; narcissism, 15, 17, 136; narcissistic personality disorder, 23–25; OCD, 46; PDD, 61–67, 118, 154; PMDD, 47; schizophrenia, 118, 154; SPECT diagnosis tool, 4; TL and, 45; warrant for, 117
mental retardation (MR), autism and, 64
methamphetamine, 74–75
MI. *See* motivational interviewing
millennials, 13, 19; blind arrogance of, 19; internal message of, 21
Miller, William R., 84
Minuchin, Salvador, 38
mood disorders, 41–49; bipolar disorder, 42, 47; cyclic, 47–48; depressive disorder, 42; dysthymic disorder, 42; statistics on, 42; treatment of, 48–49
mood stabilizers, for PDD, 67
morose type of narcissism, 17; suicide and, 17
motivational interviewing (MI), 84–90, 148; autonomy in, 85; client responsibility for change in, 85; collaboration in, 85; discrepancy development principle in, 89; empathy expression principle, 86; emphasis of, 84–85; evocation in, 85; health insurance use of, 84; medical profession use of, 84; principles of, 86–89; rolling with resistance principle of, 88; self-efficacy support principle, 87–88; for substance abuse, 84
motivation to change, 81–90; as choice, 82–83; external pressure for, 81
MR. *See* mental retardation
MRI, for autism, 65
Myers, Isabel, 95

Myers-Briggs Type Indicator (MBTI), 95–96; dichotomies of, 95–96; feedback on, 96
myths of ADHD, 51–52

narcissism, 15, 17, 136; grandiose type of, 17; morose type of, 17; problems of, 15; self-esteem movement and, 15
Narcissism Personality Inventory (NPI), 15
narcissist: diagnosable, 27–29; egocentric, 25–26; putrid core of, 29; self-loathing, 26–27
narcissistic personality disorder: DSM-IV criteria for, 24–25; NIMH on, 25; reality rejection by, 23
narcissistic rage, 28–30
National Institute on Mental Health (NIMH), 25
National Survey on Drug Use and Health, 75
natural supplements. *See* supplements
negotiation phase of contract, 122
neurological development, egocentrism and, 25
neurological research, 9
NIMH. *See* National Institute on Mental Health
NPI. *See* Narcissism Personality Inventory

object relations theory, 29
obsessive-compulsive disorder (OCD), 46
occupational scales in SII, 97
OCD. *See* obsessive-compulsive disorder
omega-3-fatty acids, 58
operant conditioning, enabling behaviors and, 34
opiates, 76–78; anxiety, depression and, 77; heroin, 77; pain management and, 76; prescription, 77; withdrawal from, 77
overfocused ADD, 55–56
overfocused anxiety/depression, 46–47; ACG, BG, DLS and, 46; eating disorders, 46; OCD and, 46; phobias, 46; PTSD, 46; symptoms of, 47

pain: of human experience, 21; management, by opiates, 76
panic attacks, 47

panic disorder temporal lobe addiction brain type, 72
parental system, failure due to, 146
parents: boundary setting, 117–118, 158; children low influence from, 18; coaching of, 143–144, 157; expectations of, 121, 122–123, 128–130, 147; feeling sorry for their children game of, 37; follow up session with, 144; goals for family empowerment, 114–115; on lack of progress to client, 136; patterns of behavior, 144; questions for, 114
PDD. *See* pervasive developmental disorders
peace, baby boomers and, 19
personality assessment, MBTI as, 95–96
pervasive developmental disorders (PDD), 61–67, 118, 154; Asperger's syndrome, 7, 61–63, 118; autism, 63–66; cognitive behavioral techniques for, 67; DSM-IV classification for, 61; ICD-10 classification for, 61; mood stabilizers for, 67; SSRI anti-depressant for, 67; ToM on, 66; treatment for, 66–67
PET Scan, for autism, 65
PFC. *See* prefrontal cortex
phobias, 46
Piaget's Theory of Cognitive Development, 25
PMDD. *See* premenstrual dysphoric disorder
positive reinforcement, 15
post-mortem studies on autism, 65
posttraumatic stress disorder (PTSD), 46
power analysis, in family empowerment, 116
prefrontal cortex (PFC): ADHD and, 51; impulsive addiction brain type and, 70–71; impulsive-compulsive addiction brain type and, 71; L-tyrosine supplement for, 58
premenstrual dysphoric disorder (PMDD), 47
prescription: amphetamine abuse, 74; opiates, 77
prison population with ADD or LD, 52
Proceeding for the Nation Academy of Sciences (Meier), 73

psychedelic drugs, 20; transpersonal psychology experimentation and, 20
PTSD. *See* posttraumatic stress disorder
pure anxiety, 43–44; BG and, 43; symptoms, 44
pure depression, 44

questions: in clinical interview, 93–95; of parents, for family empowerment, 114

reality, narcissistic personality disorder rejection of, 23
reality television, 18
ring of fire ADD, 57
Rogers, Carl, 14
Rollick, Stephen, 84
rolling with resistance principle, of MI, 88

sad addiction brain type, 71
schizophrenia, 118, 154
school, clinical interview questions on, 95. *See also* college
self-efficacy support principle, of MI, 87–88
self-esteem, lack of, 26, 29
self-esteem movement, 14; narcissism and, 15; weakness of, 14; work ethic and, 15
self-focus during emerging adulthood, 13
self-gratification of millennials, 21
self-worth, inflated sense of, 14
serotonin, St. John's wort for increased levels of, 48
Shawshank Redemption mind-set, 92
short-term goals, 106–108, 151
SII. *See* Strong Interest Inventory
Single Photon Emission Computed Tomography, 4
Skills Confidence Scale of SII, 98
social anxiety, 7, 105; in-vivo exposure therapy for, 108
social Darwinism of millennials, 21
SPECT brain imaging (Single Photon Emission Computed Tomography), 4, 55; for ADHD, 7; Amen use of, 55; on amphetamines, 75; for Asperger's syndrome, 7; for autism, 65; on marijuana effect, 73; for temporal lobe anxiety/depression, 45–46
spousal dysfunction in family, 113

SSRI. *See* anti-depressant, SSRI
St. John's wort, 58; for serotonin level increase, 48
stress: life, 42; reduction, 149; undiagnosed mental health disorders and, 7
Strong, E. K., 96
Strong Interest Inventory (SII), 95–98; basic interest scales in, 97; feedback on, 97–98; Holland codes of, 96–97; occupational scales in, 97; population for, 96; profiles for, 97; score information from, 97; Skills Confidence Scale of, 98
Stuck on Me: Missing You (Bugen), 17
student cheating, 15
substance abuse, 69–78, 153–154; ADD adults and, 44, 52; amphetamines, 74–76; of baby boomers, 20; contract and, 126; diagnosable narcissist comorbidity with, 27; family empowerment and, 116; marijuana, 72–74; MI for, 84; opiates, 76–78; treatment, 153–154
success, 157–160
suicidal ideation, 49
suicide, 27, 42; morose narcissism and, 17
superego, 26
supplements: DL phenylalanine, 58; 5-HTP, 48; GABA, 48, 58; L-tyrosine for PFC, 58; omega-3-fatty acids, 58; St. John's wort, 48, 58; strategies for ADD, 58
symptoms: of ADHD, 52–53; of cyclic mood disorders, 47–48; of overfocused anxiety/depression, 47; of pure anxiety, 44; of pure depression, 44; of temporal lobe anxiety/depression, 46

television, reality, 18
temporal lobe (TL), 45; GABA supplement for, 58; mental illness and, 45; panic disorder temporal lobe addiction brain type and, 72; SPECT scan of, 45–46
temporal lobe ADD, 55–57
temporal lobe anxiety/depression: SPECT scans for, 45–46; SSRIs aggravation of, 45; symptoms of, 46
tetrahydrocannabinol. *See* THC

theory of mind (ToM) on PDD, 66
TL. *See* temporal lobe
ToM. *See* theory of mind
transition feeling during emerging adulthood, 13
transpersonal psychology experimentation, psychedelic drugs and, 20
treatment approach, 41–42; cognitive behavioral techniques, 67; core mindfulness, 140; crisis management, 139; emotion management, 137; holistic for ADD, 57, 59; MBTI, 95–96; for mood disorders, 48–49; operant conditioning, 34; for PDD, 66–67; for substance abuse, 153–154; ToM, 66. *See also* attention deficit disorder treatment; contract; family empowerment; medication management; motivational interviewing; supplements; vocational assessment
triangulation, 38
Twinge, Jean, 15

undiagnosed ADHD, 7
undiagnosed mental health disorders, 6–7

video games/movies, violent, 18
violent behavior, 18
vocational assessment, 93–99; clinical interview for, 93–95; for directionless client, 6; Holland codes in, 96–97; MBTI, 95–96; SII, 95–98
Vohs, Kathleen D., 14

warrant, for mental illness, 117
work ethic, self-esteem movement and, 15

About the Authors

Michael D. DeVine is a licensed professional counselor supervisor who is co-owner of a private psychiatric practice in Plano, Texas. In addition to his private practice, Michael is a business consultant, advisor to local area schools/organizations, public speaker, and co-owner of the website www.onlyonebrain.com. Michael received his bachelor's degree in psychology from Otterbein University and his master's degree in psychology from the University of North Texas.

Lawrence V. Tucker, MD, is a licensed psychiatrist who is co-owner of a private psychiatric practice in Plano, Texas. He is a diplomat of the American Board of Psychiatry and Neurology, and a diplomat of the American Board of Addiction Medicine, practicing in pharmacological management of psychiatric disorders including attention deficit disorder, mood disorders, anxiety disorders, brain SPECT imaging, as well as addictionology.